Edward T Bromfield

Picturesque journeys in America of the junior united tourist club

Edward T Bromfield

Picturesque journeys in America of the junior united tourist club

ISBN/EAN: 9783744740982

Printed in Europe, USA, Canada, Australia, Japan

Cover: Foto ©Andreas Hilbeck / pixelio.de

More available books at **www.hansebooks.com**

OF

THE JUNIOR UNITED TOURIST CLUB.

EDITED BY THE

REV. EDWARD T. BROMFIELD.

PROFUSELY ILLUSTRATED.

NEW YORK:
R. WORTHINGTON, 770 BROADWAY.
1883.

PREFACE.

WHILE the following papers may be said, in a certain sense, to tell their own story, it nevertheless seems proper to make one or two preliminary statements with respect to the general plan and purport of this book.

The design has been, under cover of an imaginary class or circle of young people, led by a trusted companion or tutor, to introduce the reader to some of the most picturesque portions of our country, and to bring together such facts and sentiments from the general field of observation and reading as naturally belong to the places illustrated.

With the above purpose in his mind, the editor frankly admits that, from the first, he felt his own inefficiency, and that he feels it more keenly even now that the work, such as it is, is done. Its due performance, indeed, would seem to involve an extent and range of information and attainment far greater than that to which even his most appreciative friends could lay claim on his behalf, together with an almost superhuman faculty of condensation, owing to the strictly limited dimensions predetermined for the book. The persuasive influence of the publisher was, however, in a moment of weakness, allowed to prevail, and, having once undertaken the duty, there was nothing for it but to persevere to the end.

In respect to two of the literary features of this work (the illustrations speaking for themselves), the editor is perhaps justified in claiming some merit. He has taken conscientious pains to verify facts and dates, so that the book may be accepted as both fair and accurate, as far as it goes ; and he has sought to give it a healthful, moral, and intellectual stamp.

He may claim, also, as some justification for attempting this task, his own warm sympathies with young people. As the father of a large family, he feels, more than he can express, the importance of the season of youth, and its need of loving and timely counsel from the lips of experience, with just such helps as this and other instructive and interesting publications are designed to give. And how often does it not happen, in every intelligent home circle, that some beautiful or striking picture furnishes the text for an animated conversation, in which the appetite for knowledge is quickened, and opportunity given to correct error, and to inculcate sound and lofty sentiments! It is his earnest hope that this book may prove serviceable in these important particulars, and that, while offering some suggestions of amusement for winter evenings, it may awaken in the minds of many a love for that kind of reading which not only excites and stimulates, but strengthens and enriches the faculties of the mind.

NEW YORK, *August*, 1882.

CONTENTS.

	PAGE.
CHAPTER I.—INTRODUCTORY.	1

CHAPTER II.—THE YOSEMITE VALLEY.

Mountain Ride from Madera—Mariposa Trees and Redwoods—Peak of Inspiration—Bridal Falls—Yosemite Falls—Vernal Falls—Mirror Lake—Whittier's "Lake Side."... 4

CHAPTER III.—THE YOSEMITE.

Sir W. Scott and Bret Harte—Geological Features—Cathedral and Sentinel Rocks—North and South Domes—Boulders—Discovery of the Yosemite—Indians—Duke of Sutherland................. 17

CHAPTER IV.—CALIFORNIA AND SAN FRANCISCO.

Geographical—Early Lawlessness—1849 and 1875—City Hall and Chinese Quarter—Baron Hubner's Adventure—Seal Rocks—Pacific at Santa Clara—Trip to Silver Mine—Railroad and Cañon Scenery—Gold Mining—Glacier Moraines.. 26

CHAPTER V.—THE GREAT AMERICAN BASIN AND UTAH.

Position and Character of the Basin—Great Desert—Corrina—Rocky Mountain Slopes—Devil's Slide—Moore's Lake—Colburn's Butte—Titanic Nomenclature—Springville Cañon and the Wahsatch Range—Humboldt.. 43

CHAPTER VI.—SALT LAKE CITY AND THE MORMONS.

Approach from Ogden—Early Mormon History—Views of Salt Lake City—Mormon Endurance—Obnoxious Tenets—Polygamy and Despotism—Brigham Young—Emigrants on their Way—Dreams of Emigrants—Work and Faith—Mormon Church in Earnest—Questions for Christian Churches—Camp Douglass and the Gentiles.. 52

CHAPTER VII.—ROCKY MOUNTAIN SCENERY—SOUTH.

Daring Engineering Feats—Aspects of Colorado—The Park System—Climate—Cañons—Central City and Leadville—Gray's Peak—Garden of the Gods—Manitou—Boulder City—An Emigrant Train....... 66

CHAPTER VIII.—ROCKY MOUNTAINS AND THE YELLOWSTONE PARK.

An Extended Pic-nic—Access to the Park—The Lake—Adventure with Indians—Lower and Upper Falls—Grand Cañon—Volcanic and Glacial Action—Rock Coloring—Icebergs and Submergence—Diluvium—Drifts and Boulders... 77

CHAPTER IX.—ROCKY MOUNTAINS, YELLOWSTONE PARK, ETC.

Tower Creek Falls and Column Mountains—Hot Springs and Geysers—Chemical Action of Water and Atmosphere on Rocks—Meaning of Geyser—Explanation of Phenomena—Astounding Effects—Prismatic Coloring of Water—Earthquakes—Forces of Nature—Human Strength and Weakness—Falls of Snake River... 84

CHAPTER X.—THE PLAINS AND PRAIRIES.

Extent and Elevation of Prairies—Why No Trees—Different Theories—Letter from Settler in Nebraska—Prairie Fires—The Buffalo—Peaceful Indians—Difference between Plain and Prairie—Military Reminiscences—A Pow-wow—Indian with Scalp—Sheridan—The Indian Problem—Wapiti......... 95

Contents.

CHAPTER XI.—MOUNTAIN SCENERY IN PENNSYLVANIA.

Meaning of "Alleghany"—The Appalachians—Geological Features—Juniata and Susquehanna—Railway Cut—Sinking Spring—River of Yesterday—Kettle Run—Horse Shoe Bend—The Portage Railroads—Germans and Dutch—William Penn 108

CHAPTER XII.—THE SUSQUEHANNA AND DELAWARE RIVERS.

"Crooked River"—Lake Otsego, and Cooper—Uses and Abuses of Novels—Vale of Wyoming—Rise of the Delaware—Water Gap—The Missing Lake—Lovers' Leap—Historic Retrospect—Washington and Trenton... 121

CHAPTER XIII.—NIAGARA FALLS.

General View—Fascination and Spell—Music of Niagara—Geological Changes—Cave of the Winds and Vertical Stairs—The American Fall—Horse-Shoe Falls—Proprietary Rights—Suspension Bridge—The Whirlpool—Historical Attractions—War of 1812—"Disastrous Nonsense"—Peace of 1814..... 128

CHAPTER XIV.—LAKE SUPERIOR.

Extent and Appearance—The Pictured Rocks—Christian Nomenclature—Cascade and Great Cave—"Song of Hiawatha"—Idea and Merits of the Poem—Whittier's Eagle's Quill 139

CHAPTER XV.—BOSTON AND THE WHITE MOUNTAINS.

Boston from Bunker Hill—June 17th, 1775—A Stupid King and Haughty Counsellors—Brother against Brother—The Boston Tea Party—Taxation and Representation—Beginnings of the Dispute—"The Hub"—Fighting for a Principle—White Mountain Region—Mt. Washington—Silver Cascade—Dangers of Mountain Travel—Crawford's Notch... 146

CHAPTER XVI.—THE WHITE MOUNTAINS—CONTINUED.

The Atlantic System—Extent and Nomenclature—Franconia Mountains—Eagle Cliff—Cañon Mountains—Hawthorne—"The Great Stone Face"—Whittier's "Franconia."................................ 157

CHAPTER XVII.—OTHER PICTURESQUE VIEWS OF NEW ENGLAND.

Connecticut and the Plymouth Company—View near Granby—Why Connecticut is a small State—Mt. Ascutney, Mass.—The Missisquoi, Vt.—St. Albans—Raid and Rendezvous—Negro Head, Newport—Rhode Island and Roger Williams... 162

CHAPTER XVIII.—LAKE GEORGE.

Traveling by Imagination—The Ambuscade—Fourteen-Mile Island—General Montcalm and Fort William Henry—Sabbath Day Point—Abercrombie—Cat Mountain—Robert Rogers—War and Peace—Summer Day Glory—Whittier's "Summer by the Lakeside."................................ 171

CHAPTER XIX.—THE ADIRONDACKS.

Character of the Adirondack Region—Preston Ponds—Nature and Sadness—Lake St. Regis—Deer in the Adirondacks—The Ausable—Mr. Murray, and Trout Fishing—Lake Henderson—Upper Ausable Lake... 181

CHAPTER XX.—THE HUDSON RIVER AND THE CATSKILLS.

The Palisades, their Geology and their Uses—Notes on Major André, General Arnold, Washington Irving, and Carlyle—West Point, Tarrytown, etc., etc.—The Catskill Region—Sunset Rocks—Artist's Grotto—Rip Van Winkle—General Reflections—Conclusion.. 191

PICTURESQUE TOURS IN AMERICA.

CHAPTER I.

INTRODUCTORY.

THE JUNIOR UNITED TOURIST CLUB is an organization consisting of ten or twelve young people between the ages of fifteen and twenty, who are the regular members of the club, and a few older persons, chiefly parents of the members, who are termed "honorary members." It is not necessary for the purposes of this book to state precisely the "whereabouts" of this club. It may be assumed to be in some one of at least a hundred cities to be found on any good map of the United States. Every member of this club either has taken, or is presumed to have taken, one of the picturesque tours described in these pages. Ten very delightful evenings are supposed to have been spent in going over these tours, at the rate of one tour to an evening, under the leadership of one particular member who either by personal travel or by special reading is best qualified to take this responsible post. It is the duty of the member who leads the party to furnish sketches or engravings of the scene he proposes to describe, and every member contributes to the best of his ability to the common fund of fact, incident, and adventure thus gathered together. As some of the tours embrace journeys of thousands of miles, and the time is strictly limited to an hour and a half each evening, the reader will at once see that some very rapid traveling has been accomplished. He will also be prepared to learn (as the result of experience) that the members never seem to suffer from undue fatigue in consequence of their long journeys.

The reader is invited to consider himself, without further introduction, a corresponding member of this club, and to imagine that he hears the conversations repeated in the following pages.

The Junior United Tourist Club held its first meeting for the season, 1881–2, at the house of Mr. Merriman. The meeting was called to order by the host, and elected Gilbert Warlike chairman, *pro tem.*, and Grace Merriman, secretary.

The roll was called, and the following members answered to their names,— Albert Victor, Bertram Harvey, Clara Harvey, Cyril Merriman, Grace Merriman, John Smith, Gilbert Warlike, Kate Goldust, Laura Smith, Lilian Wiseman; also the following honorary members,—Professor Workman, Doctor Paulus, Mr. S. Harvey, Mr. Goldust, Mrs. Goldust, Mr. and Mrs. P. Merriman, Aunt Harriet Victor, Colonel and Mrs. Warlike.

Resolved: That Professor Workman be President of the J. U. T. C. Appointment accepted, and President formally inducted into the Chair.

Resolved: That the meetings of the J. U. T. C. be held weekly in rotation at the houses of the honorary members; that each meeting shall consist of (1) a short business session, (2) a conversational tour, (3) refreshments, etc.

Resolved: That the Conversational Tour be strictly limited to one hour and a half in duration.

Resolved: That the Tour for this evening be California and the Yosemite Valley, under the leadership of Miss Grace Merriman.

Resolved: That the Tour for the next meeting be the Great American Basin and Utah.

The President read the order of the evening for a Conversational Tour in California and the Yosemite Valley, and called upon Grace Merriman.

THE YOSEMITE VALLEY.

CHAPTER II.

THE YOSEMITE VALLEY.

GRACE (*reading from a MS.*) :—When papa told us at home that he was about to take mamma, Cyril, and me, for a holiday to the Pacific coast, I had only the poorest kind of an idea, in a general way, of the places we were likely to visit. Of course I was delighted, and expected to have no end of fun and excitement; but I was shamefully ignorant about the Pacific coast, except from what I had learned in the school geographies, and from reading some of Bret Harte's sketches. I must not, I suppose, go into any particulars of our journey to San Francisco, but proceed according to the programme, by giving you some particulars of our trip from that city to the Yosemite Valley, an ever-to-be-remembered event or episode in my experience, and one which sometimes seems as though it must have been a dream, so new and strange was everything. I only wish I could even faintly convey to the club the impressions I received. But I will do my best, according to the rules of the club, and I am thankful I have papa and mamma, to say nothing of Cyril, to help me through.

CYRIL: I was very observant, I assure you.

GRACE: We went by rail to a little town called Madera, and took what they call the stage to the Yosemite. There were eight of us inside, and four outside, drawn by four horses; and I shall say nothing more about this part of the journey than that it was, for more than half the distance at least, a succession of jolts and thumps up the mountains. Mamma got very nervous sometimes, and said that if this were sight seeing she had rather stay at home. Papa and Cyril were outside, and I expected every minute or two to see one or both of them plump off. We had about twelve hours of this, and were right glad at last to be summoned to dismount at Mr. Clark's ranch, part farm and part hotel, where we found rest and refreshment, and spent the night.

BIG TREES OF MARIPOSA.

The next day we devoted to the big trees of Mariposa, about sixteen miles south of the Yosemite. I am fortunate enough to have a very good drawing of the lower part of a group of these trees, and also one of a specimen of the redwood tree, belonging to the same family, but not so gigantic in its proportions.

The Mariposa grove is only three or four miles from Clark's ranch, and we rode there on mustangs or ponies. But what with looking at the trees, gathering specimens of the flowering shrubs, eating luncheon, and, if I must say so, a little mild flirtation on the part of some of our company—(here some side glances were directed toward Cyril)—the best part of a long day wore away before we alighted on the hospitable piazza of the ranch on our return. And now I must say a word or two about these same big trees, at the risk of telling you what you all very well know. Mariposa is the name of the county in California—some Indian name, I suppose—in which we are now traveling. A few years ago,—I do not know exactly what year, but probably about 1850,—when miners were prospecting everywhere along the Pacific coast for gold and other precious minerals, some of them discovered this and a few other groves of these big trees. A great stir was made about them at once, as they are of an immense size—trunks from thirty to thirty-six feet in diameter; a straight shaft, almost without leaf or branch, two hundred feet high, and then one or two hundred feet more on the top of that, throwing out enormous branches. Somehow or another the first imperfect specimens got into the hands of English botanists, and they christened the genus *Wellingtonia*, after their famous Duke; but our botanists found out that these big trees were not a family all by themselves, but had some respectable cousins called Redwood, a very familiar cone-bearing tree in California and other places on the Pacific coast. The redwoods cover an immense territory, and are used for all manner of purposes, and are very large trees too (though not so large as the big trees), forming dense forests. The botanical name of the redwood is *Sequoia sempervirens*, named in honor of an Indian chief; and so the American botanists called the big trees of Mariposa *Sequoia gigantea*, which is much more appropriate I think, than *Wellingtonia*, besides being correct.

GILBERT: What had the Duke of Wellington to do with these big trees, that Americans should be asked to call them after him? I hope the English botanists will have the good sense to drop their absurd title. The Indian name is far better.

GRACE: There are several groves of these trees on the terraces of the Sierra mountains, but nowhere else in the world, so far as is yet known. I think they are unquestionably the largest trees in the world. It is believed that they are almost as old as the Christian era, judging from the rings of the trunks.

CLARA: Are there any young *Sequoiæ* growing up, or is the race dying out?

THE PRESIDENT: A very natural question, and one which can be answered satisfactorily. The race, happily, is not dying out, as there are trees in these groves of all sizes, from the yearlings just springing up from the seeds to the hoary monsters which evidently have been in existence centuries before the Christian era. Unless destroyed by forest fires the race, though not numerous, will probably continue the pride and wonder of our western coast as long as the world lasts, or at least until far greater changes are wrought upon the surface of our planet than we can venture to pre-

REDWOOD TREE.

dict. I should say that the Eucalyptus tree of Australia, belonging to an entirely different family, is almost as large in its native forests as our *Sequoia*. By the way, Miss Clara, did you go *into* any of the hollow trees?

CLARA : Oh, of course. I went into the Pioneer's cabin, a hollow in the trunk of a tree capable of holding twelve persons; and papa rode right through one of

THE PEAK OF INSPIRATION.

the long trunks on his mustang, without lowering his head the least bit. I could tell you a great deal more about these big trees, but if we are to see the Yosemite to-night, we must make haste. And I have some very fine pictures here of some of the objects of interest.

The valley is, I think, about twenty-four miles from Clark's ranch. We go on mustangs of course. You are to suppose that it is a very hot day in June, and that there are plenty of flies. Up, up, up we go, ascending the western slopes of the Sierras, mostly through thick forests of redwood, cedar, and pine, till we come to a halting place, where we have lunch, and then on again, northward of course,

YOSEMITE VALLEY.

till we reach the verge of a mighty precipice, called the *Peak of Inspiration*, when the valley of the Yosemite bursts with all its glory upon us. Baron Hübner thus describes this view: " In front of us, on the opposite side of the Yosemite, one single immense block of square granite with a flattened summit and perpendicular flanks, rises out of the valley beneath. The Mexicans gave it the name *El Capitan*. (It is 3,300 feet from the valley bottom, and almost perpendicular.) Further on,

THE BRIDAL FALL.

towards the north-east, on both sides of the abyss, rise smooth, vertical walls of rock, diversified here and there by peaks and domes, with narrow aerial terraces,

YOSEMITE FALLS.

out of which spring gigantic firs. The horizon is bounded by a complete wall of granite, higher than the mountains which surround the valley, and of which the top appears perfectly straight. "This is the highest ridge of the Sierra Nevada."

VERNAL FALL.

I quote this because it corresponds exactly with the first impression made upon me as I looked across the valley from the peak. I do not think that either of the views I have here *quite* represents this effect, though they are admirable pictures. As we wind down from the peak into the valley, we get innumerable views, each different from the rest, and bringing new features of this wonderful scene before us. One of the first cascades we see is the *Bridal Fall*, which makes only two springs in a total leap of over 900 feet from the west side of the Cathedral Rock. We had the good fortune to see this fall at its best, as there had been very heavy rains during the spring, and the flow of water was abundant.

THE YOSEMITÉ FALLS.

LAURA: Did you notice the wave or bend in the column of water, said to be due to the current of wind striking it in its long descent?

GRACE: I did not notice that, but I understand that it is quite apparent when the body of water is not too heavy. Here is a view of the Yosemite Falls, formed by the leap of the Yosemite Creek of the river Merced, over a cliff 2,600 feet high.

JOHN: About half a mile.

GRACE: There are three leaps, of which the highest is 1,600 feet. It is estimated that when the river is full, in the spring, about a million and a half of cubic feet of water pass over this fall every hour. This is perhaps the highest fall in the world. Here is a view of the Vernal Fall, very beautiful, though not so high as some of the others, being only from 350 to 400 feet. It falls over a perpendicular rock; but steps are cut from the valley, and a brave and cool person can climb to the top if he thinks proper. At the top there is a breastwork of rock, so that one can enjoy the view without danger when once one is there. Papa and Cyril were both venturesome enough to undertake this trip. In this picture we see the breastwork to the right.

I am not keeping exactly to the order in which the visitor approaches these several sights, but I find it easier to speak of them separately. I think that one of the loveliest features of the Yosemite Valley is the Mirror Lake, embosomed among the mountains, pinnacles, and domes, and reflecting all these objects, down to the minutest lichen on the rocks, on its perfectly smooth surface. Now and then, of course, a ripple steals over the water and temporarily dispels the lovely scene. As I sat by this lake in the stillness of the afternoon, on that summer's day, while our party roamed about among the rocks, Whittier's poem, "The Lake Side," came into my mind, and I found myself repeating:

> Tired of the long day's blinding heat,
>   I rest my languid eye,
> Lake of the hills! where cool and sweet,
>   Thy sunset waters lie!
>   *   *   *   *   *
>
> So seemed it when yon hill's red crown,
>   Of old the Indian trod,

MIRROR LAKE.

And, through the sunset air, looked down
Upon the Smile of God.*

* * * * *

Thanks, O our Father! that, like him,
Thy tender love I see,
In radiant hill, and woodland dim,
And tinted sunset sea.
For not in mockery dost thou fill
Our earth with light and grace,
Thou hid'st no dark and cruel will
Behind Thy smiling face.

THE PRESIDENT: Very aptly quoted, Grace. It is not often that we find bodies of water that are sufficiently smooth and clear to give this intensely powerful reflection of surrounding objects. Some of the smaller lakes in Canada have this quality in an extraordinary degree. The water is so clear, that you can look down many feet into the depths until, as you sail along, you seem to be floating in air, and the islands and shores, lined as they are with trees, are reproduced in inexpressible vividness and beauty. But we are not yet nearly through our evening, and you have done almost all the talking so far, and I fear must be tired.

GRACE: I have finished my special talk, and am thankful to be able to call upon my brother, who kindly undertook to help me. He will, if you please, take my place for the rest of this excursion to the Yosemite, and papa will say something about California.

* Indian phrase: "Smile of the Great Spirit."

CHAPTER III.

THE YOSEMITÈ.

YRIL: When my sister spoke of the perpendicular cliff of the Vernal Falls, I had in my mind also a piece of poetry, and, to vary the entertainment a little, I will quote it, and then invite the club to guess the author's name. I should not be able to quote it correctly to-night, had I not a few minutes ago slipped into papa's library and copied the piece. Here it is:

"And now, to issue from the glen,
No pathway meets the wanderer's ken,
Unless he climb, with footing nice,
A far projecting precipice."

DR. HARVEY: If you had not said that you had copied the lines I should have credited you with the impromptu authorship; but now that I think of it, there is a certain rhythm and ring even in that short quotation which makes me think of Sir Walter Scott.*

CYRIL: You are right, sir; but if I quote the concluding lines of the stanza, their applicability to the scenes now before us, notwithstanding the disparity of circumstances, and surroundings, will, I think, be admitted by every one; names, of course, being different.

"And mountains, that like giants stand
To sentinel enchanted land.
High on the south, huge Ben-venue
Down on the lake in masses threw

---

* It is from his description of Loch Katrine—of course a much larger piece of water than the Mirror Lake of the Yosemitè, which is only a mile in circumference.

> "Crags, knolls, and mounds confusedly hurled,
> The fragments of an earlier world:
> A 'wildering forest feathered o'er
> His ruined sides and summit hoar;
> While on the north, through middle air,
> Ben-an heaved high his forehead bare."

THE PRESIDENT: Miss Grace alluded to Bret Harte in her introduction. Does any member of the club recollect his poem upon the big trees?

LAURA: I have it, sir. It is entitled "On a Cone of a Big Tree, or *Sequoia gigantea.*" He says:

> "Thy sire saw the light that shone
> On Mohammed's uplifted crescent,
> On many a royal gilded throne
> And deed forgotten in the present.
>
> "He saw the age of sacred trees,
> And Druid groves and mystic larches;
> And saw from forest domes like these
> The builder bring his Gothic arches."

His concluding thought, as expressed in the next quotation, has reference to the fact that this particular cone, instead of being the parent of other big trees, is doomed to live as a specimen upon his study table "under ink-drops idly scattered:"

> "Not thine alone the germs that fail
> The purpose of their high creation,
> If their poor tenements avail
> For worldly show and ostentation."

AUNT HARRIET: I suppose the poet would suggest to us that real practical use or progress is inconsistent with mere "worldly show and ostentation."

The Yosemitè.

Mr. Goldust: If a man or a woman gives up days and evenings to fashion and frivolity, old age, if it comes at all, will find him a mere husk.

The club cheered this proposition.

The President: I think you may now proceed, Mr. Cyril, with your narrative.

Cyril: You all know, I presume, that the Yosemitè Valley, and the Mariposa

THE CATHEDRAL.

grove, like certain other attractive parts of this country, have been set aside by sundry special Acts of Congress or State Legislation, as national parks. The Yosemitè Valley is a rift or gorge in the Sierras, possessing singularly grand and imposing features, some of which are likely to puzzle geologists for some time to come. It is about eight miles long, by about a mile broad, of irregular shape, but hemmed in through its entire length by lofty granite hills, nearly vertical. The river Merced runs through the valley, with tributaries flowing into it from both

THE SENTINEL ROCK.

sides, and constituting the various waterfalls, to some of which reference has been made. The floor of the valley is about 4,000 feet above the level of the sea, and the hills tower up from 2,000 to 6,000 feet above the plain. The valley itself is richly wooded, and in summer is carpeted with grass and wild flowers. The latest suggestion as to its formation is that it was caused by a sudden depression of the earth's surface —a caprice of nature. No other theory, like that, for instance, of aqueous erosion, or fissure, or glacial action, can, it is thought, explain the almost total absence of débris at the foot of the hills. Occasionally there are rock avalanches, when great portions of granite are detached and fall with a thundering crash to the plains; but there is every reason to believe that where they have fallen they remain to this day, which would not have been the case had there been any glacial disturbance, or the rushing of a vast body of water for centuries through this gorge. Do I put this correctly, Mr. President?

The President: Yes. It is supposed by many that the gorge was at one time a lake, and that it has been gradually filled to its present level by the falling masses from above.

Mr. Goldust: How long will it take to fill it up by this means?

The President: We cannot tell what sudden changes may happen to hasten

THE NORTH AND SOUTH DOMES.

the comparatively slow action of climate, storm, and gravitation; but we might safely put it at thousands of years.

Mr. Goldust: Then there will be a chance for all the club to visit the place yet.

Cyril: One of the most prominent objects in the valley (we are going north) is a group called Cathedral Rocks, about 2,660 feet high, and from some points of view presenting a church-like and very imposing appearance. Above this is the Sentinel Rock, a weird and solitary peak, or rather group, 4,500 feet high.

Below the Yosemitè Falls are the mighty North and South Domes, the latter of which has hitherto defied all attempts made by travelers to climb it. The sketch of rocks and bowlders gives an idea of some portions of the valley along the course of the Merced, not far from the base of the South Dome, and it illustrates the President's remark about the rock avalanches. Another sketch gives us a nearer view of the South Dome.

THE PRESIDENT: We have not heard yet about the discovery of this valley.

ROCKS AND BOWLDERS IN THE VALLEY.

CYRIL: I had forgotten to say that in 1851 an expedition was organized by the miners in the Sierras and Foot Hills, to pursue and punish the Indians for various outrages they had perpetrated upon the whites. The Indians fled to their fastnesses, and, amongst other hiding places, this one was discovered, and the unfortunate Red Men were attacked, and great numbers slaughtered in this very spot. A few years later, tourists began to visit it, and in 1856 the first hotel or ranch was built there. The name is Indian, of course, and signifies "grizzly bear." The Indians in California now give little or no trouble to the whites. The tourist meets with them occasionally, but they are harmless. In the Yosemitè region they are known as Digger Indians.

MR. GOLDUST: How did you get out of the valley? Did you take all your party up the precipice at the Vernal Falls, or return by the way you entered?

THE SOUTH DOME.

CYRIL: There is a rugged and steep way out in a northerly direction. Some tourists, indeed, enter from this direction. As you ascend from the valley, the air grows perceptibly cooler. In fact, the whole region is subject to sudden changes of temperature, and to severe storms. Cool nights and hot days alternate with each other. Our party got thoroughly drenched in a rain storm on the road to Coulterville; but, after we had proceeded a few miles, our clothing dried upon us, and we thought no more of it. Some carriages were waiting for us at the first point in the road available for wheels, and some of our party gladly changed their method of locomotion, though I do not think they gained much by it, as the roads are

FRIENDLY INDIAN.

not smooth by any means, and in some places the driver has to proceed very warily, or he would upset his party into some deep ravine or abyss. Coulterville is a small mining town, and the tourist will be in no humor to remain there longer than necessary to recover from his fatigue. From Coulterville we drove some forty miles down the rugged slope, into the plains, to the line of the railroad, and so on the following day reached San Francisco.

AUNT HARRIET: I have been very lately reading a description of the Yosemitè Valley by Dr. Russell, one of a party accompanying the Duke of Sutherland last June in a rapid tour through the States and Canada. A friend of mine in London sent me a copy of the work.* Dr. Russell says: "The peculiar and unique feature of the valley seems to me to be the height and boldness of the cliffs, which spring out from the mountain sides like sentinels to watch and ward over the secrets of the gorge. Next to that is the number and height of the waterfalls ; but it is only by degrees and by comparison that the mind takes in the fact that the cliffs are not hundreds but thousands of feet high—that these bright, flashing, fleecy cataracts fall for thousands of feet." He adds : "What is the use of rolling off a catalogue of names and figures? Even the brush of the painter, charged with the truest colors and guided by the finest hand and eye, could never do justice to these cliffs and waterfalls."

CYRIL: I had almost forgotten to say that the Duke of Sutherland and his party preceded us by only two or three weeks. We heard a great deal about them from the guides and others. It appears that some of the party, including the Duke himself, were very much amused by a guide calling upon the Duke to help him water the horses. "Here, Mister Sutherland, hold this bucket, please, while I pump." There was a good laugh, but the Duke obeyed with alacrity.

GRACE: I rather liked to hear the story. I do not suppose the man meant to annoy the Duke, and it was a reminder to him, anyhow, that dukes and lords do not grow out here.

GILBERT: Perhaps that is why our people run after them so much when they do come.

KATE: Well, people cannot help being born heirs to dukes and duchesses. I do not know that I should have been so very sorry if I had been a duchess.

AUNT HARRIET: An American girl who is true to herself needs no title to proclaim her nobility.

* An American edition has been published.

CHAPTER IV.

CALIFORNIA AND SAN FRANCISCO.

THE PRESIDENT called upon Mr. Merriman, who promptly took the part of leader of the club for the concluding portion of the Californian tour.

Let me first, he observed, give a general idea of San Francisco. It is situated at the northern end of a peninsula thirty miles long and about six wide. The city slopes towards the east, facing San Francisco Bay, which is between thirty and forty miles long, and from seven to twelve miles wide. The entrance to this bay from the Pacific Ocean is through the Golden Gate a strait, five miles long and a mile wide. The shores of the Golden Gate are picturesque, the northern being lined with lofty hills. The bar has thirty feet of water at low tide, and the bay has safe anchorage for ships of any size.

In 1846, San Francisco was a mere fishing-hamlet. Gold was discovered in 1848, and in less than four years the city had a population of 35,000. It now numbers at least a quarter of a million.

On the eastern shore of the bay, opposite San Francisco, is the city of Oakland, bearing a somewhat similar relation to it that Brooklyn does to New York, only that Oakland is relatively more fashionable, and is even more thoroughly a residential city and suburb than Brooklyn.

The ferryboats plying between these two cities are mammoth boats, with immense saloons above the deck. The distance is seven miles.

It gives one a strange feeling to walk the busy and beautiful streets of San Francisco and Oakland, and to think that all this has sprung up in far less than an average life-time. There must be many men now living who can look back to the time when it was an unpretentious hamlet, and when no one dreamed of the future before it.

California and San Francisco.

During the early years of the city, things proceeded after a very lawless fashion. The people who flocked to it were influenced by only one motive, and that a powerful one—the thirst for gold. There was no strong government to restrain the unruly and punish crime. At length the inhabitants formed a Vigilance Committee, which soon became " a terror to evil doers," even if not " a praise to those who did well." Its decisions were prompt, and its punishments severe, though perhaps not always just. It was not until 1855 that the municipal government

THE BAY OF SAN FRANCISCO.

and the regular tribunals of justice became strong enough to cope with the situation; but by that time a new element had sprung up in the city—a class of men who lived by trade and commerce, as well as by mining, who were in themselves a guarantee of good order, and to whom, on the other hand, good order and permanence in the institutions of government were indispensable. Still the population of the city is so heterogeneous, and the rowdy element so strong, that it continues to have its full share of crimes and disturbances, perhaps rather more so in proportion to its population than the other large western cities.

I must not, however, be betrayed into giving you a merely statistical narrative. Here is a series of sketches which, without any words, would convey a very good idea of the Capital of California.

DR. PAULUS: When I visited San Francisco, I was particularly struck with the contrast between its climate and that of the eastern cities of America. It was decidedly cooler in the summer months than I have ever known it to be in New

SAN FRANCISCO, 1849.

York, and I understand that it is warmer in winter. We found the climate of California very variable.

MRS. PAULUS: Yes, and there seemed to be constant fogs in San Francisco.

MR. MERRIMAN: During the summer months the prevailing winds are from the northwest, and the cold air current, striking against the coast range, generates a vapor which accumulates in clouds and mists. But, for all that, the Pacific coast is much sought after by invalids. In summer, many people leave San Francisco for Oakland, and other points on the main land, which are also considered desirable places for consumptives. I should have said that Oakland is the stopping-place of the Central Pacific Railroad. The bay, of which a partial view is given in our sketch, is a beautiful sea. On a clear day the view across it from the upper streets of San Francisco is singularly fine.

The streets of San Francisco are very irregular. The plan of the city is modeled after that of nearly all other American cities—straight lines and right angles,—but the irregularities of the ground are such that a good deal of engineering has been called into requisition to preserve even a moderate consistency in this arrangement. Steep hills, terraces, and in some places steps, which forbid

BIRDS-EYE VIEW OF SAN FRANCISCO, 1875.

carriage access in that direction, are quite common. This is owing to a large part of the town being built upon the side of a granite mountain.

The view of Montgomery street, the Broadway of San Francisco, gives an excellent idea of this. Here the crowd is more cosmopolitan than even in New York. All nationalities are represented, the Chinaman especially being noticeable. They are an industrious and thriving people, living in a section of the city by themselves, and numbering many thousands. I was amused by reading a description of a traveler's adventures in this part of San Francisco:

"One night," says Baron Hübner, "I was returning to my hotel after an agreeable visit, and being, as I thought, sure of my way, I refused the escort of my host. 'Turn round the Chinese quarter,' was said to me, and off I started. But the night was dark; a damp, penetrating fog added to the obscurity; and in San Francisco, from Germany to China is but a step. All of a sudden I find myself in a narrow, dirty street, evidently inhabited by the yellow race. I hurry my steps, but in the wrong direction, and here I am in the very midst of the Chinese quarter. As far as the thick darkness will allow me to judge, the streets are completely deserted. The houses are wrapped in sombre shadow. Here and there, red paper lanterns swing from balconies. At every step I stumble against the sign board, and hear whispering inside the houses, where the presence of a stranger has thus been betrayed. In some places the darkness is complete, and I can only go on by feeling. In others, momentary and vivid lights creep along the woodwork of the gilt shop shutters, and light up some grotesque monster, or the cabalistic red

NEW CITY HALL, SAN FRANCISCO.

and black letters on one of the sign boards. The wind increases in violence: driven by the gusts, the clouds and fog sweep down into the street and hide even the stones. I pass by an open door; a feeble light streams from it; I hear the sound of voices and dice; it is a gambling-house. A man placed as sentinel seems glued to the wall. He evidently takes me for a police inspector, and rushes in to give the alarm. I hurry on as quickly as I dare over the slippery steps. I begin to see at my feet one of the broad cross-streets of the lower town. At this very moment, at the corner of a blind alley, I am attacked by a band of women. These harpies hang on to my clothes, seize me with their horrid, bony fingers and nails like birds' claws, and peer at me with faces besmeared with white, red, and yellow paint. Fighting my way as best I can, I at last manage to rid myself of them, and followed by their screams and imprecations—luckily their mutilated feet prevented their running after me—I reach civilization, my face

THE CHINESE QUARTER, SAN FRANCISCO.

streaming with perspiration, and in half an hour more I arrive safely at my hotel."

Mr. Goldust : The Baron was fortunate to get off so easily.

Clara : Are all the Chinese people bad and depraved in San Francisco?

Mr. Goldust : By no manner of means. Some of them are highly reputable and wealthy merchants. But as a class the Chinese are dealt rather hardly by,

MONTGOMERY STREET, SAN FRANCISCO.

and it is no wonder that the more brutish among them retaliate upon the white man wherever an opportunity presents itself. Besides, the Chinese quarter in San Francisco is under very poor police supervision.

Mr. Merriman : The picture of the Seal Rocks represents a very curious scene which the San Franciscan shows to all his friends. It is a view from the

SEAL ROCKS.

Cliff House, a hotel about six miles from the city, connected therewith by a wide boulevard. The outlook is towards the Pacific Ocean—and a glorious outlook it is. In the foreground are these rocks, upon which the sea-lions or seals make their holiday, wriggling and clambering up the sides of the rocks after a fashion which partakes of the marvelous.

THE PRESIDENT: It is now time for us to hear something about other portions of California.

MR. MERRIMAN: With pleasure. Here is a view of the Pacific from the coast of Santa Clara county, some forty miles below San Francisco county. The capital of this county is San José, a thriving city of some fifteen to twenty thousand inhabitants. It has some remarkably fine public buildings and parks, and the climate of the whole region is mild and equable. As all sea views are very much alike, we will now pass into the interior, and I will ask my daughter to describe a visit we paid to a silver-mine in Virginia City, Nevada. It is a little beyond the confines of California, but near enough to give us a general idea of mining operations in this part of the world.

CLARA: Instead of giving you my own description I shall do what will be much better, namely, read you a portion of the description of the same journey made by a lady who accompanied us, and recently published in *Lippincott's Magazine*. The writer says:

"It is a bright, clear day, warm as June in the sun—(it was August)—cold as March in the shade, with a brisk, sharp breeze from the bay, blowing the white powdery lime-like dust full in one's face; just such a day, in short, as can be found for eight months of the year in San Francisco, when during a morning stroll you are sure to meet dusters and ulsters, lace shawls and seal-skin jackets; the wearers apparently utterly oblivious as to what season it really is. * * * The Valejo boat is reached, and we steam out into the bay, surrounded, as one generally is in every California steamer, train, or stage, by *commis voyageurs* of a decidedly Jewish cast of countenance. Looking back across the rippling, blue water, we catch one last glimpse of the town, half shrouded in a soft, golden mist. Farewell, great city of contrasts, of the very rich and the very poor; of the Irish millionaire and the Chinese beggar, of the palace and the gambling-hell; of the breezy hill-top, and the low opium-scented valley.

THE PACIFIC OCEAN AT SANTA CLARA.

"The sun is setting, and the golden mist which we left hanging over the city like a soft bright canopy, is creeping after us when we reach Vallejo, and take our places in the train for Virginia City. Our friends, the Israelitish *commis voyageurs*, have dispersed, and in their place we have tall, bearded men, with their wives. They are, one and all, without a single exception, talking stocks.

"Early the next morning we leave the sleeper, and, after depositing our bags and shawl straps with the baggage master at Reno, start empty handed for Virginia City. During the night we have come through the ever green Sacramento Valley, but now we strike northward, straight up into the Sierras. All vegetation, except an occasional patch of yellow tar-weed, is left far below us. The great mountain slopes, bare and brown as we near them, but softly purple in the distance, and the clear brilliant blue of the summer sky, are all that we see. The road, twisting and turning as the ascent grows ever steeper, lies so close along the mountain side that at times it seems as if nothing but a miracle could keep us from plunging into the valley, many hundred feet below. * * * Now and then we rush past deserted villages, where the frail, shell-like wooden shanties are already falling into decay. Again, we stop at the station of some small hamlet—city by courtesy—perched on the bare hillside, and composed of half a dozen miner's huts, an equal number of saloons and billiard-rooms, and the railroad station."

At last Virginia City is reached, built on the side of a hill, and looking, in spite of its large houses, "as if a very slight push would send it reeling into the valley." The party, after the usual California lunch of mutton-stew and pork-and-beans, proceeded to the mine.

"Following our guide, we entered a large building filled with rapidly revolving wheels of every size, some of which are used to work the elevator running constantly up and down the main shaft; while others move the immense pump which forces the cool air from above into the mine.

"Each of us having been provided with a bundle of rough-looking garments, we are ushered into the ladies' dressing room."

At last the party are properly equipped and begin the descent.

"At first I can do nothing but grasp my companion's arm. Then comes a sensation of floating, but upward, not downward, and it is not until I see by the light of the lanterns that we are passing passage after passage cut in the granite walls, and each one lower than the last, that I fully realize the fact that every moment is bringing us nearer the center of the earth. Almost before I have collected my senses, we stop at the mouth of a large cavern, and I hear W——'s voice sounding as if many miles away, so deaf have I become by the sudden change of atmosphere, at 1,750 feet below Virginia City.

"From several points run narrow arched passages furnished each with a

SILVER CITY, NEVADA.

railway on which the ore-cars are brought to the elevator, and into one of these black openings we plunge. On and on, through the heat and darkness, now slipping as we step by chance on iron rails, now passing a huge pipe connected with the air pump, now standing close against the shining, dripping walls, to let pass a low, heavy car loaded with ore, and pushed by a couple of miners; then on again, until we come to a small circular cave, the walls composed of heavy beams of timber closely packed together, but bent in more than one spot by the tremendous pressure from above. Some of the richest ore has been found here; and a little farther on we come upon a group of men at work. There is a small pool of water to be crossed by means of a narrow plank, and then, one, two, three ladders to be climbed, the heat becoming more intense at every step, until we reach a niche-like opening where two men are at work — or, rather, where one man works for a quarter of an hour, while the other sits with his arms in a pail of ice-water.

TRESTLE BRIDGE NEAR SACRAMENTO CITY.

"The descent of those frightful ladders is, if possible, more perilous than the ascent. We follow our guides up one passage and down another, till a heavy curtain, which hangs from wall to wall, is pushed aside, and a hot blast seems to scorch our very bones. From that moment each step is one of increasing agony. I feel as if the whole seventeen hundred and fifty feet of earth above me were resting on my chest; my blood, which seems on fire, is driven violently to my head, and as each fresh wave of heat passes over us I gasp painfully for breath. The next ten minutes will always be a haunting memory to me. The long, dark passages, the burning atmosphere, the scattered lights, the weird figures of the miners, appearing only to vanish the next moment in the surrounding gloom, all recur like some terrible dream. * * * After thanking our guide, we get on the elevator and, warmly enveloped in pea-jackets, return once more to the upper air."

TALULOWEHACK CAÑON, SIERRAS.

Albert: The great wealth of Nevada is in its silver mines. The famous Comstock lode is partly beneath Virginia City.

The President: I see that we have a sketch of Silver City, which might be, by its looks, the scene of several of Bret Harte's stories—"Smith's Pocket," for instance. I know no better way of familiarizing oneself with the peculiarities of this wonderful section of our country than by reading Bret Harte.' Take, for instance, his graphic description of a snow-bound party in the Sierras in "The Outcasts of Poker Flat." This is suggested to me by the picture before me of Talulowehack Cañon. Imagine winter setting in suddenly, as it always does, in such a scene, and a party of outcasts snow-bound at the foot of one of those hills.

SNOW-SHED, CENTRAL PACIFIC RAILROAD.

Mrs. Merriman: Do you think Bret Harte a good writer?

The President: Decidedly. He is not a romance writer, but he is far better than that, he is a graphic and trustworthy artist. He paints men and things as they are, or have been, and accordingly his works will increase in literary value with every generation.

Mr. Merriman: I would like to hear Mr. Goldust give us some information about gold-mining in California.

Mr. Goldust : I have been so much interested that I ought not to refuse to contribute a little to the fund of entertainment. You all know that I have lived twenty-five years and more in California. I went there in 1856, a poor man. I became interested in gold-mining, and have been rich and poor alternately on an

A CALIFORNIAN MINER.

average every three years. Fortunately I have been able to retire at last from active business, and unless I become tired of traveling, or doing nothing, shall in future carefully avoid all mining speculations, or speculations of any kind. I have been looking at the sketch of a Californian miner, and I can only say that it reminds me of some of my earlier days. I worked hard I assure you to get my first capital out of the dust of the earth.

LILIAN : What are those men doing?

MR. GOLDUST : The man holding the hose is directing two powerful hydraulic streams against the rock to loosen the earth and so cause it to wash down the sluice. The other man in the picture is shoveling the loosened gravel or earth into the sluice, from which, by various mechanical or chemical contrivances, the gold is finally extracted.

THE PRESIDENT: It is now time for the club to take its departure from the land of the Sierras. I invite you, therefore, to take your places in the train. The journey is long and not destitute of interest or of peril. You will be thankful to pass in safety over the long trestle bridges across the creeks in the Sacramento Valley, and will duly admire the snow-sheds and deep cuttings through which you are traveling at the moderate pace of twenty-two miles per hour.

GRACE : I intended to state that there is an interesting article on the Coniferous Forests of the Sierra Nevada in the *Century Magazine* for last September (1881). The writer says that these forests are the noblest and most beautiful on earth, though, owing to the shortness of the time which has elapsed since their discovery, they are as yet but little known. He asserts that the soils on which the forests are growing are in fact glacier moraines, that is, soil deposited by the ice glaciers after being crushed and ground from the solid flanks of the mountains. I would like to know something more about these glacier moraines, and the action of ice in preparing beds for the growth of these immense forests.

THE PRESIDENT : We have not time this evening to go into so large and interesting a subject, but it will certainly come before us again, and your curiosity may then be gratified. I have read the article you speak of with great interest, and consider it an excellent contribution to the natural history of this region.

The proceedings of the club then assumed an informal character.

CHAPTER V.

THE GREAT AMERICAN BASIN AND UTAH.

THE second meeting of the J. U. T. C. was held at the house of Dr. Paulus. Every member was present, and also several invited guests.

The routine business having been disposed of, the President invited Dr. Paulus to conduct the club through its second tour.

DR. PAULUS: If you look at the map of America, you will find on the western portion two lofty mountain chains or systems. One is comparatively close to the Pacific Coast, and includes the Coast range and the Sierra, which, though separated by an extensive and rich valley, may be regarded for our present purpose as one system; the other is the great Rocky Mountain system, running from the extreme north to the peninsula. Between these two mountain systems is a vast undulating and broken valley, called by geographers the Great American Basin.

KATE: A very matter of fact name.

JOHN: German *bach*, brook, or place of flowing water: geographically, a dip on the surface.

DR. PAULUS: We are now descending into this Great Basin on its western side, hastening down the Sierra's slopes as fast as the railroad people think it prudent to draw us. Remember, however, that the Great American Basin, though it includes the whole of Nevada, and parts of Utah, Arizona, and California, is far surpassed in extent by the basin or valley of the Mississippi, which lies to the east of the Rocky Mountains. Indeed, geographers not uncommonly ignore, as it were, the Great American Basin, by including all the three mountain systems of which I have spoken—the Rocky Mountains, the Sierra, and the Coast range—in one grand system, which they speak of as the Rocky Mountains, or Pacific coast range, in opposition to the great Appalachian or Eastern mountain system. But for the present we have to do with this great valley, and not with the whole of it either.

We have some picturesque views here which will help us in some degree to understand what this valley or basin is like. It is by no means uniform in its features, but presents almost infinite variety of physical aspect, and is at present the scene of some of the strangest developments in human character and history.

THE PRESIDENT: Will Dr. Paulus mention some of the special geological and physical features of this Basin ?

DR. PAULUS : I presume you refer to the peculiarity that it is what I may term self-drained. None of its rivers seem to have any outlet towards the sea. The region, however, abounds in lakes, in some of which the water is salt. These lakes

GREAT AMERICAN DESERT.

receive the rivers, but in consequence of the little rainfall and the great evaporation they rarely have any outlet—the Great Salt Lake, for instance ; or, if they have, the stream is usually soon absorbed in the earth.

JOHN : I understand that this region, though comparatively depressed, is an elevated plateau, with ranges of hills running through it, generally north and south.

DR. PAULUS : Yes, and these hills are of a volcanic origin, treeless, and rain is gradually washing their substance down into the valleys. But enough of these preliminaries. That portion of this Great Basin we are now entering is very peculiar, and to the eye unattractive. It is termed the Great American Desert, and is applied especially to a tract of land some seventy to one hundred miles square,

The Great American Basin and Utah.

though of very irregular outline, and apparently utterly profitless and barren, both in an agricultural and mineral sense. In traveling through this region the eye sees only bare, brown hills and plains, covered with sand and alkali, with a thin growth of sage-bush, and grass. There is no water visible. Special trains convey this necessary commodity daily to the different stations along the railroad. In wet weather the soil becomes like mortar, and traveling, except by the railroad, is well nigh impossible.

LILIAN: Does sage grow out in this desert? I should think that there must be good soil in it somewhere.

THE PRESIDENT: It is not the garden sage, nor anything like it. The sagebush is a species of *Artemisia*, the wormwood group of the order *Compositæ*. It seems indigenous to these dry alkaline soils, and as it is a shrubby plant, it makes good fire-wood in these regions.

DR. PAULUS: We are now entering, if you please, the confines of Utah territory.

GRACE: The land of Blue-beards.

DR. PAULUS: Most of

CORINNA.

it, unfortunately, is held by the Mormons; but they will not interfere with us, though we may have a little to say about them by and by. Here is Corinna, not a Mormon town, though in Utah.

KATE: It does not look much of a place.

DR. PAULUS: No, nor very picturesque; but it is a specimen of a frontier city, and has a large trade with the great mining regions of this great Basin. At Ogden City we leave the Union Pacific for the Utah railroad for Salt Lake City. But before going there, I wish you to look at some beautiful views of Utah scenery, after which we shall have something to say about Mormondom.

THE DEVIL'S SLIDE.

I have said that a portion of Utah is in the Great Basin. But as we approach Ogden we get nearer glimpses of the lofty Rocky Mountains; in fact we begin to ascend the slope on the east side of the basin. Here the railroad track sometimes winds along the bottom of a wild ravine. " Cañons, now gloomy and savage, then radiant in verdant beauty, run up into the mountains. Waterfalls come tumbling from dizzy heights. Huge masses of rock, torn and splintered into grotesque shapes, seem to have been fashioned by the fantastic caprices of genii, rather than by the unaided operations of nature." One of the most remarkable of these rock formations is known as the " Devil's Slide," of which we have a view. There is a hill, or rather mass of dark red sandstone, some eight hundred feet high. Up the side of this,

MOORE'S LAKE, UTAH.

from base to summit, runs a stratum of white limestone consisting of a smooth floor about fifteen feet wide, on either side of which is a wall varying from ten to thirty feet in height. As seen from the railroad it resembles a huge mass of masonry, and it is very difficult to discover by what natural agency it has been produced.

Some five years ago a celebrated artist visited some of the most picturesque portions of Utah, and painted some remarkably beautiful pictures. Amongst other places he sketched was Moore's Lake, of which I am able to give you an engraving. This lake is eleven thousand feet above the sea level. It is about nine miles in circumference. It lies about sixty miles south of the railroad among the Uintah Mountains. The water of this lake, as might be supposed from its altitude, is always very cool. It is generally thought that this region has been the center of great glacial rivers. Around the shores of Moore's Lake the mountains rise abruptly to a height of three thousand feet and more, and from the top of one of them there is a view on a clear day of over twelve thousand square miles. There is abundance of timber and very fine pasturage. The lake evidently gets its supply from the melting snows. We are now in the region of cañons—

THE PRESIDENT: Pardon me for a moment. Miss Laura, what is the derivation of the word cañon?

LAURA: I looked that up, and also the word butte, which is used to describe the high, pinnacle-like, isolated peaks common in this western mountain scenery. Cañon is from the Spanish, pronounced canyon, and signifies originally a tube or pipe to carry off water. We use it in this country to designate the deep, mountain, rocky rifts or ravines, with precipitous sides, which are so numerous and also so grand and beautiful in our mountain regions.

THE PRESIDENT: And "butte?"

LAURA: Butte is from the French, and means a high, bold hill. It is pronounced, I suppose, as one syllable, and the "u" should be short.

THE PRESIDENT: Thank you.

DR. PAULUS: One of our illustrations is of Springville Cañon, which is in the Wahsatch range, directly on the verge of the Great Basin. It certainly gives one an idea of loneliness and desolation, though of grandeur likewise. This cañon is not far from a Mormon town of the same name, on the southeast border of Utah

Lake, a large fresh-water lake flowing into the great Salt Lake. We see here plainly the action of the water in cutting this enormous and gloomy rift in the mountain side. You can look down upon the little stream from a point fifteen hundred feet above it. And I understand that this cañon is only a specimen of many similar ones throughout this grand mountainous region. Laura has spoken of the word butte as descriptive of certain hills. Some of these are strange and awful monuments. Immense masses of rock, a thousand or two thousand feet high, perhaps, sides almost perpendicular, and looking like compact and solid towers of masonry built by a Titanic race of men.

THE PRESIDENT: Favor us, Albert, with the key to the word "Titanic."

ALBERT: I imagine it refers to the Titans of Greek mythology, a fabled race of giants, far back away from any historic period, powerful enough to make war against Jupiter.

THE PRESIDENT: Whenever a vast, gloomy, and awe-inspiring object is before us it is natural to think of the traditional heathen stories of the freaks of this race of giants, hurling mountains at the gods.

AUNT HARRIET: I suppose that in all ages and among all races of men the love of the marvelous and the idea of the supernatural have been prominent characteristics. And especially do we seem to find everywhere the idea of a rebellious race at war with the ruling powers of the universe. I wonder whether the idea of these Titans has any affinity as to its origin with Genesis 6: 4–7.

THE PRESIDENT: It is not improbable, as we see a strange though often a grotesque and weird likeness to Scripture history in many heathen traditions. I think that Frederick Von Schlegel brings out this thought very clearly in his Philosophy of History. By universal agreement of ancient traditional sources this world was early the scene of a great conflict between opposing moral influences.

MR. GOLDUST: To judge by the frequency of the references to his Satanic Majesty in the nomenclature of the picturesque and grand objects in creation, that personage must have had no little influence in this world. There is hardly a square mile of mountainous country but has some point named after him.

THE PRESIDENT: In the Golden age of Grecian mythology, man is said to have lived in peace and plenty, and in happy communion with the gods; but this was succeeded by a degenerate or Silver age, in which the passions of men became turbulent

SPRINGVILLE CAÑON.

and wicked. Then followed the Brazen age, in which crime and disorder reached its highest pitch. This was the age of the Titans, and of their war against the gods, which issued in the triumph of the latter. But the Grecian mythology does not embrace the idea of an elevation or restoration of mankind. It gives us the Iron age as the closing term of human degeneracy, and there it leaves us. The idea of malevolent supernatural influences being at work among men, fostering this evil spirit of disobedience, and causing grand and awful disturbances in the physical world, to the dismay and destruction of mankind, is universal. It has been reserved for the Christian system to bring out the truth of a divine fatherhood and rulership of love, through whom and through which the devout may find safety 'amid the wreck of matter and the crash of worlds.'

MR. MERRIMAN: Utah is much more picturesque in its physical features than I supposed.

DR. PAULUS: It is divided into two sections by the Wahsatch Mountains which form part of the eastern slope of the Great Basin. The waters which flow westward find no outlet to the ocean for reasons which I have explained. The Wahsatch range is grand and full of features of interest. The Uintah range is also very picturesque, with towering peaks covered with perpetual snow. For extreme diversity of scenery and climate, this part of the United States is almost without parallel.

ALBERT: It will be a long time before the Great Basin becomes populous.

DR. PAULUS: Portions of it will never become so, but it has, as we have seen, great mineral wealth locked up within it, and some of it is already finding its outlet.

KATE: Perhaps the rivers which now sink into it may some day find their way out also.

DR. PAULUS: At Humboldt wells there are about thirty springs, some of which have been sounded over 500 yards without touching bottom. As these springs rise to the surface it is supposed that they may be the outlet of some vast subterranean lake. But the surrounding region is most desolate, and, I agree with Albert, not likely to attract visitors at present, although it is thought that the Humboldt valley might be made productive by irrigation. Being the highway between East and West, this valley may become, in the near future, more attractive for labor and settlement.

CHAPTER VI.

SALT LAKE CITY AND THE MORMONS.

MR. PAULUS: I have here a series of views of Salt Lake City. This place lies, so to speak, on the eastern edge of the Great Basin, at the westerly foot of a spur of the Wahsatch Mountains. We approach the city from Ogden, by the Utah Central Railroad, which follows the eastern shores of the Great Salt Lake. Salt Lake City is about twelve miles from the southern extremity of the lake. The first view shows the Wahsatch Mountains to the left or east, so that we are looking south. The second view is from a point southeast of the city, and therefore looking northwest, with the lake in the background. This is the point from which Brigham Young first saw the valley which was to be his future home, and the chief city of his deluded followers. And here I will ask my friend Bertram to relate to us some of the particulars which led to that memorable journey of Brigham Young. I know that he has been studying the history of this remarkable heresy, and can probably furnish the club with a brief summary of the leading incidents.

BERTRAM: I will do my best. The founder of the Mormon sect, as everybody knows, was Joe Smith, who brought out his book of Mormon in 1830, and in the same year organized the Mormon Church. He was an infamous man, notwithstanding his claims to be the leader of a religious sect; he tried his hand at banking, and cheated his depositors, and was otherwise disreputable. The Mormon Church removed its headquarters from place to place, being compelled to "move on" by the authorities and public sentiment. The irregularities mostly charged against them were burning and plundering houses, and secret assassinations. They were a kind of Ishmaelitish people, and were suspected of all kinds of crimes and misdeeds. At last, I think in 1839, they concentrated to the number of seven or eight thousand in Illinois, and built a city which they called Nauvoo, in Hancock County. They obtained a charter from the State, which permitted them to organize a little army, and Smith became a general, as well as a self-styled prophet and apostle. For a time his authority was supreme in Nauvoo, and the Mormon Church increased rapidly, but at length his immoralities stirred up a spirit of hatred and revenge among his people, and some of them appealed to the State for protection. This led to a kind of civil war. Smith and his brother were captured and put in jail at Carthage, but the jail was attacked by an infuriated mob, and both were shot dead. Of course Mormon affairs were thrown into great confusion, out of which they were extricated by Brigham Young, who had been a rising man for some time in the

SALT LAKE CITY FROM ENSIGN PEAK.

sect, and now put in a formal claim for the presidency of the Church and was chosen to that office. The State very properly revoked the charter of Nauvoo, and Young conceived the plan of emigrating to some far off place where the Mormons would be likely to be undisturbed for a great number of years. He prospected around in the vast region of the Rocky Mountains, and at last, in 1847, fixed upon the site of a city, and the Mormons, who had been having a hard time of it at Nauvoo, flocked thither to a man, and laid the foundations of the city.

DR. PAULUS : Admirably sketched, Mr. Bertram. And now I will do the Mormons the justice to say that their emigration or exodus from Illinois to Salt Lake

SALT LAKE CITY.

was one of the most remarkable events of the kind in the history of the world. The distance traveled was 1,500 miles and more. They had to journey in wagons, on horseback, on foot, through a region uninhabited and waste. They crossed the great prairies, ascended the mountains, penetrated the deserts, and defiled through the numerous cañons. They endured indescribable hardships, and many died on the way; and even when they reached their journey's end they found no welcome awaiting them; not even the shelter of forests and the luxury of a well-watered valley. For years they had to live on the hardest of fare, and often to suffer hunger, thirst, and cold, without the means of providing sufficiently for their most necessary wants. But they had faith in their leader, and at last they conquered the desert; they brought water from the mountain lakes in perpetual streams and brooks into their valley; they built themselves homes, and in fact established themselves as a people and a State. However abhorrent and detestable some of their principles and practices are, history will do them the justice of acknowledging the magnitude of the deed they accomplished.

THE PRESIDENT: I would suggest, doctor, that you state some of the objectionable principles held by the Mormons, so that before we leave this subject we may have a fair view of the case as a whole.

DR. PAULUS: Certainly: and in doing so I would carefully discriminate between the mere errors and delusions of Mormon faith, and those principles and practices which bring it into unceasing and essential antagonism with Christian civilization. As to the pretended revelations of Joe Smith, and all the mockery and mimicry of the apostleship, the civil state or government has nothing to do with such things. It has no right to interfere, for the constitution of this country expressly provides for the fullest enjoyment of religious liberty compatible with the general laws of morality which the nation as a whole has inherited, and which enter into the spirit of the commonwealth. The most conspicuous and obnoxious tenet of the Mormon Church is its inculcation of polygamy.

ALBERT: Do they not base this upon the practices of the patriarchs?

DR. PAULUS: Certainly; but Christian civilization, as founded on the New Testament and the teachings of Jesus Christ, discountenances polygamy, as opposed to the highest interests of mankind, and as ruinous to the proper claims and rights of womanhood.

CLARA : Lady Duffus Hardy, in her book " Through Cities and Prairie Lands," narrates a conversation with a Mormon railroad conductor on the Salt Lake City line, who says that there are many Mormons who never dream of taking more than one wife.

BERTRAM : And she also says that the women have been trained from childhood to believe that polygamy is right, and that the natural rebellion they feel is regarded by them as the voice of the evil one, to be stilled only by prayers and self-mortification.

MRS. WARLIKE : I should like to have the making of laws for Utah for the next ten years. I would make it rather hot for these polygamous husbands.

DR. PAULUS : Another obnoxious principle of the Mormon Church is its claim over the consciences and lives of its followers, ordering them to undertake services in its behalf, to their peril and danger; sentencing them to death if their offenses come within the range of such extreme penalty; doing all this, not in open tribunals and in accordance with the principles of law and order, but secretly, despotically, in defiance of personal rights and liberties, and often in violation of law. Christian civilization has an extreme horror of secret tribunals. It believes in law and publicity, and in the rights of conscience and of the individual citizen. These two features of the Mormon Church—polygamy and secret irresponsible despotism—bring it into direct opposition with the enlightened public sentiment of this country and, I may say, of Christendom.

COL. WARLIKE : It is a kind of expanded and rampant papacy, with a jesuitical taint of the rankest and most dangerous complexion.

DR. PAULUS : Undoubtedly. Purify the Mormon Church of these two maladies, and the nation will not quarrel with them about their eccentricities of belief, and they may remain in Utah to all time. As it is, there is a ripple, and perhaps more, of public sentiment among the strict Mormons of a new exodus to some region even yet beyond the borders of Christian settlement, or possibly to a country where their practices may be less repugnant to public sentiment. But it is time for us to proceed on our journey, or at any rate to look around us a little in this strange place.

Very different the scenes presented in these pictures to those which greeted the eye of Brigham Young and his companions in 1847—thirty-five years ago.

Here we have a very beautiful city, well wooded, richly watered, and bearing all manner of fruits in her enclosed orchards and gardens; with the added charm of mountain scenery, and the proximity of a noble inland sea. The city, which is the capital of Salt Lake county, as well as of the territory of Utah, is large, populous, and beautiful. It is laid out in blocks of six hundred and sixty feet square, separated by streets one hundred and twenty-eight feet wide. Ditches or cuttings run through most of the streets, on both sides, filled with water brought from a distance. Most of the streets are lined with handsome trees. The houses are generally built of adobe, and are of but one story. Some are very large and handsome, and

THE HAREM AND THE RESIDENCE OF BRIGHAM YOUNG.

all have gardens. The public buildings are not numerous, nor very imposing. The Tabernacle, with its peculiar dome-like roof, will seat fifteen thousand persons. Besides this, the Mormons are building an immense temple. There are a number of smaller places of Mormon worship, a few "Gentile" churches, banks, etc. The most conspicuous private dwelling is the house which Brigham Young occupied. It is rather a collection of houses than a house, and is still occupied, in part, by his numerous widows and their families. We have also in our collection a portrait of Brigham Young as he appeared when nearly seventy years of age—a remarkably well preserved man, one would say, though with a cunning expression in his countenance, which is far from attractive.

Salt Lake City and the Mormons. 59

Main Street is the chief business street, as its name implies, and to the visitor presents a unique picture. There are no trees on this street, and the houses are built close to the sidewalks. The style of architecture of the different houses varies considerably, but many of the edifices have considerable claims to notice, and are quite worthy of an Eastern city. At times this street is thronged with bullock wagons, coaches, and carriages of every description, together with miners, Indians, and the residents of the city, passing to and fro, or engaged in shopping.

JOHN: What is the staple trade or industry of Salt Lake City?

DR. PAULUS: It is the leading trade center of the territory, which is fairly rich in mines of lead, silver, copper, and gold. There are also coal-mines. A surplus of agricultural produce comes to market, and there has been a steady advance in manufactures.

Here is a picture of Mormon emigrants on their way to Salt Lake City. From the beginning of the settlement, Brigham Young relied for recruits chiefly upon foreign countries. In England and Wales, Australia, and on the continent of Europe, the Mormon missionaries have for years been busy in the work of proselytizing. Scarcely a rural village in England, and more particularly in Wales, but has been the scene of this kind of preaching; and many of them have yielded converts. These are invariably from the poorest and most ignorant of the population, to whom the word-pictures, skillfully drawn, of the paradise awaiting them in America, if they will but join their fortunes with the faithful, present a vivid contrast with the life of toil and penury to which they seem inevitably

BRIGHAM YOUNG.

doomed in the land of their birth. These missionaries are skillful in adapting their appeals to the varied conditions of their auditors. Their object is to get men and women and children. The necessary funds are supplied by the Mormon Church —the principal use to which the contributions and tithes of the "faithful" are devoted. Here is a fine company on their way to the promised land—fathers and mothers, young men and young women, boys and girls. You do not see any old or decrepit people. They have encamped on a spot which overlooks the valley of the Salt Lake, though at a great distance, and with eager, longing hearts they are striving to get a glimpse of the blessed place! Every one has his or her own

MAIN STREET IN SALT LAKE CITY.

vision of prospective happiness. All the visions are not alike, but they are all tinged with a rosy hue. There is work before them, but there is plenty also, and abounding delights and comforts which will be to them a present and palpable pledge of the bliss which they will enjoy in the life to come. Mormonism is essentially materialistic in its views of things. The Mormon idea of God is of a Being of flesh and blood. Jesus Christ is His Son. Man has existed from all eternity, and the future life, in some other world, will be but a continuance of beings holding the same relations as they do here, and similarly constituted. No wonder that this group of people is characterized by such an aspect of hopefulness and of joyous anticipation as manifests itself on every countenance and in every bodily attitude.

MORMON EMIGRANTS ON THEIR WAY TO SALT LAKE CITY.

I think that the artist has been very skillful in giving this character to the picture.

Arrived at their destination, a convenient camping place is found for them, while the bishops and heads of the church go around and ascertain the capabilities and the history of each person. Work is found for all. The idea of letting the new arrivals drift helplessly along, or entering into a contest for existence without

"WORK AND FAITH." MORMONS WORKING AT THE GRANITE FOR THE TEMPLE.

guidance, is not to be thought of. Unfortunate, indeed, it is, that all this wonderful executive talent is at the service and in the cause of so infamous a system as that of Mormonism.

THE PRESIDENT: I have often wondered at the superiority of many of the methods and plans in furtherance of evil systems over those which are put into operation by good men for good purposes. As a rule, the churches of Christendom take no interest whatever in advancing the material interests of their people. They will contribute and bestow money in charity, but the general plan is to let men severely alone, to struggle in life as best they may, without sympathy or guidance, unless they come as paupers for charity, and then they are stamped at once as degraded. Why should not Christian churches in America do the work for humanity which Mormonism only pretends to do? Why should a Mormon emigration system succeed, while the planting of a Rugby Colony becomes abortive of the good intended? Why should Christian communities sit by in luxury, seeing Christian men contend against superior forces, when a little practical sympathy would save many a valu-

CAMP DOUGLASS.

able life, and people many a desert region? It is not only charity for the sick and help for the victims of some special calamity, or the care of a few miserable street Arabs, that Christianity enjoins upon us; it is brotherly sympathy of man for men —the union of forces against the common enemy.

DR. PAULUS: I cannot attempt to answer those pertinent questions. The subject is one that deserves the most practical thoughts of our wisest men and women. Here is a suggestion in the picture "Work and Faith." See how from the granitic mountain sides are hewn out the massive stones to be shaped and polished for the great Mormon temple. So, from the mountain masses of humanity may be shaped the polished stones for the spiritual palace of the skies. Nothing can be achieved without toil, but faith is needed to sustain the toiler; otherwise he sinks into the gloom, sooner or later, of utter despair.

The idea of the Mormon Church is to interest itself (for its own welfare chiefly) in every new comer. Work, food, social companionship, are found for all. Money is advanced to those who enter upon farming. It is secured by mortgages, and becomes often a permanent burden; but meanwhile there is a visible means of support, and poverty, in the sense in which that word is understood in populous

SALT LAKE.

communities elsewhere, is unknown. The Mormon farmer may be heavily in debt to his church, but somehow he thrives very well and is more than content.

GILBERT: Suppose a Mormon should be converted back again to Christianity, can he get away easily from his new associations?

DR. PAULUS: I understand that the conversion of a Mormon is a very rare event. They are under a grip which never relaxes its hold. And there are secret laws against perverts, which the Church does not hesitate to put into execution, so that it is highly dangerous for any one to renounce Mormonism after having once embraced it. But, notwithstanding this, I have an idea that Mormonism cannot withstand the moral forces which accompany an aggressive Christian civilization. Already a large proportion of the residents of Utah are "gentiles," and if, in the progress of settlement, the latter should become the numerical majority, Mormonism must gradually change its character or disappear.

The last picture in this group is of the military camp at Fort Douglass, where the United States government maintains a force of soldiers. It was with extreme reluctance that the Mormons admitted the right of the government to establish this fort, but they had finally to submit. Whether with a prompt demonstration of military power the Mormon Church could be made to abandon her obnoxious tenets and practices is a question upon which the country is deeply agitated at the present moment. Many think that the cancer has been allowed to exist too long already, and that, like slavery, it will now require a very vigorous application of the knife to remove it. There have grown up political complications around this question which make it a difficult matter for the Executive to move ; and yet it is generally felt that the crisis is near at hand, and that firmness above all things is now necessary on the part of the government. But we have not time to discuss the Mormon question, and I shall cheerfully give place now to my friend Bertram, who is to give us some further light and help over this Rocky Mountain region.

CHAPTER VII.

ROCKY MOUNTAIN SCENERY—SOUTH.

BERTRAM: I shall have to take you away from the overland railroad, and invite you to perform some rapid journeys with me, as I lead you to some picturesque scenes to the south of the line in the State of Colorado.

Before we leave the track, however, look at this view of a railroad bridge over one of the creeks or valleys in the Great Basin. The engineers of the old world are fairly astonished at the daring of our engineers on this side of the world, with whom it often becomes a necessity to accomplish feats which could never enter their heads if they were constructing railroads in countries of a less bold physical contour, or with unlimited means at their command. In this case, for example, the railroad has to cross a chasm of perhaps a quarter of a mile in width, and several hundred feet in depth. No time nor money for elaborate masonry! The thing has to be done quickly, cheaply, and, withal, effectively. This leads to a close study of the possibilities of timber, and the result is a bridge which, under inspection, is pronounced perfectly safe for travel. Occasionally, of course, a collapse takes place, and one hears of engineers rushing their trains at full speed across a rickety bridge and seeing it fall to pieces behind them as they just reach the opposite side. Whether such a thing has ever really happened, or is simply a feat of imagination by story writers, I cannot say; but we all know that not long ago what was thought to be a very solid bridge over the river Tay, in Scotland, collapsed suddenly while a train was passing over it, and that train and passengers disappeared into the abyss. On the whole, the timber bridges of America have stood the test of experience remarkably well, I think.

KATE: Hübner says that the last sensation of fear in the journey from the Rocky Mountains westward is the peril of passing over the trestle-work bridges near Sacramento City. I suppose this remark would apply in general to trestle-work bridges everywhere. The greater the abyss to be crossed, of course the greater the apparent peril.

Here is a picture giving one a general idea of the comformation of cañon scenery in Colorado.

THE PRESIDENT: Will some member of the club be good enough to furnish us with a few geographical and other points about Colorado? Perhaps you are prepared to do this, Bertram.

BERTRAM: I have collected a few particulars. Colorado is about 380 miles east and west, by about 280 miles north and south, and is almost a parallelogram in shape. Geographically it may be said to have three natural divisions—the mountains, the foot-hills, and the plains. The mountains intersect the territory north and south, and have many branches and spurs. In the center of this mountain region, behind the peaks seen from Denver, are what are called the Parks, a series of immense picturesque valleys bounded by mountain elevations. Of these the principal are, the North Park, with an area of 2,500 square miles; Middle Park, 3,000 square miles; South Park, 2,200 square miles, and St. Luis Park, nearly as large as all the other three put together. There are many other smaller parks scattered all through this mountain system.

BRIDGE OVER A CREEK.

MR. GOLDUST: These parks would dwarf the noblest of the magnificent parks surrounding the palaces of the titled aristocracy of the old world. What scope is there not in these regions for human energy, and what a future may there not be for a country so richly gifted!

BERTRAM : Of course, if I were to invite you to a walk or a ride round one of

CAÑON SCENERY IN COLORADO.

these gigantic parks, you might reasonably decline the invitation. Here, however, is a little sketch of Middle Park, which gives a good general idea of these "pleasure grounds of the gods." The foot-hills, averaging 7,000 or 8,000 feet in altitude,

GRAND CAÑON.

lie to the east of the mountains, and slope towards the plains, the latter consisting of a series of valleys and ridges traversed by many streams, and with an elevation above the sea of about six thousand feet. West of the Rocky Mountains is the easterly side of what we understand as the Great Basin.

The parks are watered by numerous small streams, the head waters of the larger rivers. They are most interesting regions for the geologist, and are full of mineral springs of very valuable medicinal properties. The climate of Colorado is said to be remarkably healthy, with mild winters and cool summers. The high mountains are, of course, to be excepted. The atmosphere also is peculiarly rare, invigorating, and tonic in its quality. The pasturage is excellent and capable of sustaining vast herds of stock, and this industry is progressing very rapidly.

MIDDLE PARK.

Another of the remarkable features of Colorado scenery is its cañons. Some of these are within view from the cars of the railroad. Here is the Grand cañon of the Colorado, where the river cuts its way through many miles of solid granite, in some places 7,000 feet high.

The Clear Creek cañon is on the Colorado Central Railroad. This gorge is so narrow that in many places the torrent which roars along the bottom fills up the whole space. Often the mountains seem to close in upon its tortuous windings, so as to leave no possibility of exit, till by some sudden turn a passage is discovered. Far overhead are peaks covered by eternal snows. And yet, through this cañon the railroad is constructed—a narrow-gauge line, of course—following the windings of the ravine, and with the sharpest of sharp curves.

VIEW OF CLEAR CREEK CAÑON, COLORADO.

This road is not, however, built for pleasure purposes merely. It traverses a rich mining district.

Mr. Goldust: The streets of Central City are paved with the refuse from the gold-mines, and as the ore has been only imperfectly worked they may be said to be literally paved with gold.

Kate: Is not Leadville somewhere in this region?

Mr. Goldust: Leadville is on the Southern Colorado Railroad, 279 miles from Denver, and the center of the Colorado silver-mining district.

It has sprung up into prominence and wealth within less than five years. Only the most recent editions of the encyclopædias contain any reference whatever to it, and yet to-day it is a stalwart young city of some twenty thousand inhabitants. It is in the heart of a rich silver-mining district, and of course has attracted to itself not only enterprise and capital, but a vast amount of the ruffianism and lawlessness of the nation.

GRAY'S PEAK.

BERTRAM: Here is a pretty view of Gray's Peak from Middle Park. The snow-capped mountain in the far distance is Gray's Peak, and the stream running through the center of the picture is the Grand River. Gray's Peak is 14,251 feet above the sea level.

MRS. GOLDUST: Is not the "Garden of the Gods" somewhere in Colorado?

BERTRAM: Yes. I have not any pictures of it but it is the name given to a little park or valley near Colorado Springs. It is about five hundred acres in extent, and is shut in by mountains on the north, west, and east. The entrance to it is through a narrow defile called the Beautiful Gate, and it contains some curious rocks of red and white sandstone, of great height and of singular appearance. These, I imagine, are "The Gods" which

BOULDER CAÑON.

suggested to some fanciful tourist this strange name. The surroundings are romantic.

We are not far from the famous Manitou Springs, situated near the base of

Pike's Peak, and much frequented by invalids, especially asthmatics and consumptives. It is about five miles from Colorado Springs. It is the correct thing to ascend Pike's Peak from this town, and from the summit of this mountain, nearly 15,000 feet above the sea, the views are among the grandest in the world.

And now, if you please, we will find our way to Boulder, a small mining town. Near this place is a mountain gorge called Boulder Cañon, which we must visit. We must go in carriages, as the cañon is seventeen miles long, and the walls rise precipitously in some places to a height of 3,000 feet. A stream rushes down the cañon, crossed in many places by the wagon road. This cañon differs from many others in that, while preserving almost unrivaled features of grandeur, there is an entire absence of gloom. The roadside is decked with flowers in the summer season, and the eye is refreshed by the infinite variety of rock and dell and ver-

BOULDER CAÑON. THE FALLS.

IN FOREST TRAIN.

dant foliage. This place is a great health resort for the people of Denver, who stoutly maintain that the Yosemite Valley, Niagara Falls, Delaware Water-gap, and European Alpine scenery are tame and commonplace when compared with the scenery of Boulder Cañon.

Mr. MERRIMAN : Traveling in Colorado does not seem to be very difficult, judging from the quickness with which we manage to transport ourselves from place to place.

BERTRAM : Of course we are specially privileged, as with us time and distance are annihilated and we travel on the wings of the wind. But, as a matter of fact, the development of the railroads in Colorado within the past few years is one of the most wonderful features of that wonderful land. They are all narrow-gauge, of course, but they seem to laugh at engineering obstacles. They pierce through the narrowest ravines and ascend the steepest mountains with an audacity that compels admiration. I understand that the civil engineers constructing the narrow-gauge lines in Hindostan, sent a representative to inspect the Colorado lines, and have followed many of the plans adopted by the latter.

I have preserved two sketches showing different views of the celebrated Boulder Cañon. My last sketch tells its own story. I cannot define the exact position of this cañon, but it is a vivid picture of many a weary, patient pilgrimage through these rocky defiles and mountainous solitudes. Let us wish the travelers a safe journey and a prosperous future.

The time for closing the conversation having now arrived, the proceedings became informal, and, in due season, the club adjourned, to meet in a week's time at the house of Mrs. Victor.

CHAPTER VIII.

ROCKY MOUNTAINS AND THE YELLOWSTONE PARK.

THE third tour, namely, a trip to the famous Yellowstone Valley, was the subject of a conversation by the Club at the residence of Mrs. Victor, who had undertaken the duty of leadership on the occasion.

The preliminary session of business was soon over, and Mrs. Victor began as follows:

I do not know whether to be sorry or glad that it has fallen to my lot to lead this Club to the wonderful region of the Yellowstone Park. Lady Duffus Hardy, in writing of the Sierras and Pacific Coast mountain region, enthusiastically says: "To all those who are in search of health, of novelty, and who are able to enjoy the noblest, the grandest, and most varied scenery this world can boast, I would say, 'Go westward, across the Rocky Mountains, the glorious Sierras, and sit down at the Golden Gate." I would take the liberty of adding—Do not omit the journey to the great National Park of the Yellowstone.

We start, if you please, from Ogden, and travel north to Virginia City—not the Virginia City of Nevada, of which we heard on a previous evening, but its deserted and forlorn namesake of Montana. Here we provide ourselves, being a large party, with guides, mules, and all the necessary paraphernalia of a camp, for a long journey is before us. Or we can go by stage to the lower Geyser Basin on Madison River—it takes the better part of two days to do this—and make our headquarters at a hotel there. We can find there horses, guides, and all necessaries for our explorations.

THE PRESIDENT: It is an extended picnic, I presume.

MRS. VICTOR: Indeed it is. Remember that the Yellowstone Park is sixty-five miles one way by fifty miles another. We have a good deal before us, I assure you. I need hardly say that we have chosen the month of August for our trip, as the region is now in its full summer glory, and traveling is unimpeded by the snows; a very important consideration, as we may be detained ten or fifteen days sight-seeing in this locality.

As we have to compress this into a single evening on this occasion, I shall not go into the minute and hourly details of our journey, but simply take up such points of interest as are sketched for us in these beautiful pictures.

Here is a charming view of Yellowstone Lake, a magnificent sheet of water, of varied outline, but averaging say twenty-two miles by about twelve. It is seven

YELLOWSTONE LAKE.

thousand seven hundred and eighty-eight feet above the sea, and the surrounding hills rise from three thousand feet to five thousand feet higher. The physical contour of these hills is very romantic. The lake is deep and the waters clear as crystal. The guides say that there is excellent salmon trout fishing in its waters. Now please remember that this is the highest lake in North America. There is only one lake on the whole continent that has a higher elevation. I forget the name.

CLARA: I can tell you; Lake Titicaca, in South America.

MRS. VICTOR: It is glorious to stand on the shores of this lake in its wild solitude, and think that we are upon the dividing ridge of this great country of ours. Fed by the snows and springs of this region, and by the stream of the Upper Yellowstone from the south-east, it sends forth from its northern shores the noble Yellowstone River, the main tributary of the Missouri, while from the adjacent hills burst forth streams which flow westward and southward, and empty themselves in the California Gulf, or the Pacific Ocean.

JOHN: Is this lake always smooth and limpid?

MRS. VICTOR: Towards evening, as the mountain breezes blow upon it, its surface becomes rough, and like all mountain lakes it is of course subject to occasional storms. But the general aspect of the lake during the summer is calm and peaceful.

KATE: I wish to ask, at this point, why you enter the valley from the north or north-west, instead of from the south?

MRS. VICTOR: The Yellowstone Valley is walled in on all sides by stupendous mountains, and those in lower Wyoming to the south are particularly difficult of transit.

GILBERT: I see smoke to the left in the mid-distance on this picture of the lake.

MRS. VICTOR: Probably from forest fires, most of which result from carelessness on the part of travelers.

GILBERT: Are there Indians in this region?

MRS. VICTOR: Oh yes. There is a large Indian reservation in Wyoming. Speaking of Indians, I read in a recent number of *Appleton's Magazine* of a rather romantic adventure with the Indians in Yellowstone Park. There was a party of four, two gentlemen tourists, a guide, and a soldier from Fort Ellis. Suddenly the guide detected a cloud of dust far away to the south, which he said must indicate the proximity of Indians. By-and-by the Indians came nearer. The rifles were made ready, but as the savages approached they made signs which meant peace. They were four in number, and the writer says that four more picturesque savages could not have been desired to lend romance to the situation. One had on a bright blue coat faced with scarlet. All were well armed with rifles. They said, in broken English, that they were going to a council up in Montana. Subsequently the travelers learned that the tribes of the Utes, to which these

THE LOWER FALLS.

Indians belonged, had just broken out into a revolt, massacred an agent and a number of soldiers, and were decidedly on the war path.

MR. GOLDUST: In this case ignorance was perhaps bliss to the travelers. They would have been rather uneasy if they had known all the facts.

MR. MERRIMAN: People do not get their daily papers regularly away up in these wilds.

MRS. VICTOR: Our next view is of the Lower Falls. Their height or rather depth is three hundred and sixty feet, and they are inexpressibly and grandly beautiful. I should say that they are situated about fifteen miles from the northern extremity of the lake. About a quarter of a mile from the Lower Falls are the Upper Falls, with a depth of one hundred and forty feet; and just before these are a series of beautiful rapids.

We now prepare to enter the Grand Cañon, an immense chasm or cleft, with its walls from a thousand to fifteen hundred feet high, from which the river seems to wind along at the bottom like a silver thread. We have a picture here showing a portion of this cañon, with the Lower Falls in the distance. The Grand Cañon is twenty miles in length, so that you see we have a long task before us to explore it. And here I would ask the Professor to favor us with some information about the geological features of this wonderful gorge.

THE PRESIDENT: I have never visited the Yellowstone Valley, and am not a

CLIFFS IN THE GRAND CANON.

professional geologist, and cannot, therefore, offer you any original views on the subject; but from all I have read about it, including the reports of Professor Hayden, the government surveyor, and others, there seems to be no doubt that this wonderful region has been the scene both of volcanic and glacial action of a remarkable kind. The volcanic forces are evident to this day to the most casual observer in the immense collections of hot springs, and the powerful geysers which form some of the principal objects of interest, and about which, I suppose, we shall hear something from Mrs. Victor by-and-by. The solid rocks themselves are also, many of them, of a volcanic nature, consisting of lava which has been belched forth age after age. Ridges of basaltic rocks have been cut through by the rapid streams. There can be no doubting this testimony, and other evidences furnished by the rocks, which are eloquent and truthful witnesses to the earnest and laborious student of nature as to the events of the immense past. The very coloring on the sides of the cañons, so marked and brilliant, is evidently due to the action of water at a boiling temperature ejected from numberless springs over the surface and percolating in every direction.

KATE: Perhaps it was this peculiar coloring of the rocks in this valley that gave to it the name of Yellowstone.

THE PRESIDENT: Not unlikely, though I have not met with any authoritative explanation upon that point. The action of ice, however, in the cañons of the whole of this Rocky Mountain region is also clearly traceable. There was a period, no doubt, when the temperate zone on this continent was subject to much more intense and continued cold than it now experiences. But even to-day the present existence of glaciers, or vast moving masses of ice, forcing themselves through ravines or gorges, and carrying with them boulders and detritus from higher regions, is demonstrated. These cañons of the Yellowstone have evidently been subjected to this experience. Vast blocks of crystalline rocks are perched upon the basaltic strata, ten and fifteen hundred feet from the bottom of the gorge. And there are proofs enough in the general arrangement of the mounds of detritus on the plains and along the bases of the hills to warrant the inference that ice has been the great carrier.

DR. PAULUS: Do not some geologists think that at one period the whole of this northern continent was submerged, and that the distribution of unstratified rocks is due to the action of icebergs?

THE PRESIDENT: That was the theory first propounded by Sir Charles Lyell, but the study of terrestrial glacial action of late years affords us data sufficient to account for the phenomena we are now referring to without calling upon the action of water at all. At the same time there are, in other places—for instance, on the eastern parts of this continent—very palpable proofs that either during or since the deposit of glacial drift the region has been submerged, allowing for the deposit of more recent strata, of clays and sands overlying the drift. But we must not branch off into this interesting topic.

MRS. VICTOR: I am greatly obliged to you for your explanations.

BERTRAM: One word more on this subject of glaciers. I have been trying to conceive how the ice gets into these mountain gorges, if, as you say, they were not filled with water.

THE PRESIDENT: Oh, yes, I ought to have said that these regions were then, of course, regions of perpetual snow. The snow would in time pack the ravines, and by simple pressure would be changed into ice. This process is going on in the Alps, and in other regions of perpetual snow, at this moment. The whole subject of glacial development is one of great interest.

LAURA: Is there a limit to this glacial action on the earth's surface, or is it more or less noticeable all over the world?

THE PRESIDENT: I believe that no traces of diluvium or glacier drift are found in the tropical regions. They are seen, however, in the southern hemisphere, where, of course, the flow is from the south pole, northward.

ALBERT: Are the Colorado cañons of the same nature, geologically, as these of Wyoming?

THE PRESIDENT: Generally speaking I may say they are; that is to say, the nucleus is granitic or igneous, there has been free volcanic disturbance, and the evidences of glacial action to the limits of the temperate zone are abundant. But I fear we shall drift away from our topic, if we do not mind.

KATE: Call it a geological drift.

JOHN: Never mind, if we get at some boulders of thought or knowledge.

THE PRESIDENT: Mrs. Victor, it is your turn, if you please.

MRS. VICTOR: Then suppose we begin another chapter.

CHAPTER IX.

THE ROCKY MOUNTAINS, YELLOWSTONE PARK, ETC.

MRS. VICTOR : We will now leave the Grand Cañon, grateful for all the suggestions it offers us as to the great changes that are taking place on this globe of ours, and proceed to inspect the beautiful Tower Creek Falls. Tower Creek is a small tributary of the Yellowstone, flowing through a ravine which, I am sorry to say, has a Titanic stamp upon it, in its name—the Devil's den. The falls have a height of 156 feet, and the creek at their base runs through a romantic glen to the main river. The pictures will describe this better than any words of mine.

And now, after just a peep at the Lower Cañon, about which much could be said descriptively if we had time, I will proceed to the Geyser districts of the Yellowstone. These are classified into two divisions, the calcareous hot springs of Gardiner's River at the north of the Park, and the upper and lower geyer basins of the Madison River, farther to the south and west of Madison Lake. Here is a view of the hot springs on Gardiner's River. The club will look at it while I tell them all I know about it.

CYRIL : The artist has had the good sense to introduce two people—members of the J. U. T. C. I suppose—in the foreground. One has a large portfolio under his arm.

MRS. VICTOR : You may imagine a river falling over a series of steep rapids—down, down it goes, terrace after terrace ; only instead of being simple terraces they are hollowed into basins, of different sizes, giving to the terraces a very irregular appearance. The water comes from an almost innumerable number of hot springs—thousands of them—which form themselves into a stream, and then rush over the declivity in the manner shown in the picture. When the water issues from the springs it is very hot. It fills the little reservoirs on the terraces, and in

TOWER CREEK, BELOW THE FALLS.

each leaves, of course, a residuum of lime or silica. As you look at this cataract from a distance, it gives you the idea of an irregular white wall. It looks, indeed, like a mass of snow and ice. Columns of steam rise up from it here and there, and towards the foot of the declivity the water becomes cool enough for people to bathe in it. Those basins into which the water no longer flows are crumbling away into a calcareous powder; but where the water still flows, the rims of the basins are constantly replenished with wavy, frill-like borders of all kinds of vivid colors. There are evidences of many

TOWER FALLS AND COLUMN MOUNTAINS.

hot springs which have stopped flowing, and it is supposed that there is a gradual diminution of the volume of water falling over these terraces.

KATE: How large are these basins?

MRS. VICTOR: Averaging perhaps five or six feet in diameter and two or three feet in depth. The total depth of the descent is about two hundred feet. There are some larger basins on the top of the terrace, one of forty feet in diameter, and twenty-five feet deep. The white appearance of the cascade suggested the name of

"White Mountain Hot Springs" to this locality. I believe a good many people visit the Parks for the purpose of bathing in these springs for purposes of health.

HOT SPRINGS.

BERTRAM: What causes the vivid coloring you speak of on the rims of these basins?

MRS. VICTOR: That I do not know.

THE PRESIDENT: It is due to the chemical properties of the water and the action of the atmosphere. Prof. Hayden says that as the water flows along the valley it lays down in its course a pavement more beautiful and elaborate in its adornment than art has ever yet conceived. The sulphur and the iron, with the green microscopic vegetations, tint the whole with an illumination of which no decorative painter has ever dreamed.

Mrs. Victor: But I must now show you the Geysers.

Kate: What is the origin of that word?

Laura: The dictionary will tell you that, Kate. Icelandic, *geysa*, to burst forth violently. You know that these peculiar fountains were first discovered in Iceland. But I would like you to tell me what causes the hot water to burst out of these springs.

Kate: I am afraid I must plead ignorance.

The President: I think Bertram has been reading on this subject. Perhaps he will tell us all about it.

Bertram: I do not know that I quite understand what little I have read, but I suppose that in some way these deep and large springs or underground reservoirs of water become heated—by volcanic heat, whatever that is—and that the steam forces itself into the tube connecting them with the surface, where the water of course is cooler. The steam is condensed, but the water in the tube increases in temperature, and is raised higher and higher by successive pressures of the steam below, until the water in the basin ceases to act as a condenser, and the steam and boiling water are forced up through the tube, as they are out of the spout and lid of a kettle, until the reservoir is exhausted for the time being—until as we may say, the water has all boiled away. Then the springs gradually refill, and the process is repeated.

The President: Very well explained, I think; and I may add that the reason all the hot springs are not geysers is that they do not all happen to build up by their deposits a vertical tube high enough to hold a column of water to keep these boiling springs in check until they have accumulated sufficient force to make a violent demonstration. The nature of the soil, therefore, in which these springs occur may have something to do with the matter.

Mrs. Victor: Whatever the cause or theory, the effect is astounding, for a district of twenty or thirty square miles is pretty thickly covered with these geysers, large and small; and what with the springs themselves boiling and bubbling and bursting out in this peculiar way at intervals, together with the weird aspect of the ground, covered with silicious and calcareous deposits, and the crater-like

THE GIANTESS GEYSER.

mounds of all sizes, one feels, indeed in a land of marvels. Some of them send up volumes of water over two hundred feet in height, and with steam a thousand feet high, the irruption lasting several minutes. Here is the Giantess Geyser and some others, surprising a party of visitors, who I must say look anything but dignified.

LAURA : I suppose there is a Giant Geyser, as this is a Giantess.

MRS. VICTOR : Oh yes ! And it has been known to be in irruption for three hours at a time, but its volume of water is not so high nor so beautiful as the Giantess. Then there is the Grand Geyser, the Castle Geyser, the Old Faithful Gey-

GROTTO GEYSER.

ser, so called because of the regularity of its outbursts, about once every hour, the Turban Geyser, and hosts of others; making this district of the Yellowstone Park the most wonderful in the world for this kind of natural phenomena. Here is a small view of the Grotto Geyser with a dome-like crater and numerous apertures.

THE PRESIDENT : Of the Castle Geyser, Professor Hayden writes : " It is the most imposing geyser formation in the valley, and receives its name from its resemblance to the ruins of a fortress. The deposited silver has crystallized in immense globular masses, like spongiform corals. The mound is forty feet high, and the lower portion rises in steps." Speaking of the prismatic coloring of the water he says: "About the middle of the day, when the bright rays descend nearly vertically, and a slight breeze makes just a ripple on the surface, the colors exceed comparison; when the surface is calm there is one vast chaos of colors, dancing, as it were, like the colors of a kaleidoscope. As seen through this marvelous play of colors, the decorations on the sides of the basin are lighted up with a wild, weird beauty, which wafts one at once into the land of enchantment: all the brilliant feats of fairies and genii in the Arabian Nights' Entertainments are forgotten in

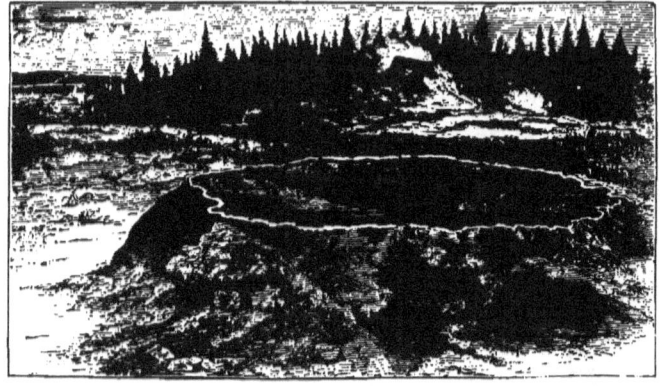

CASTLE GEYSER AND FIRE BASIN.

the actual presence of such marvelous beauty; life becomes a privilege and a blessing after one has seen and felt its cunning skill."

MRS. MERRIMAN: I think I shall move that when we adjourn for the season we do so to meet next August in the Park of the Yellowstone.

MRS. VICTOR: I was going to say that all this volcanic energy so near the surface is suggestive of earthquakes, which occasionally take place in this region.

KATE: Then I object. I had rather do my sight-seeing in this way.

MR. GOLDUST: People on the Pacific coast, which is occasionally visited by earthquakes, do not dread them more than the people in the Eastern States dread thunder-storms, nor do I think they do nearly so much damage.

AUNT HARRIET: I sometimes think that it is a mercy we are not left to live and die without some evidences of the mighty and awful forces in the universe.

MRS. WARLIKE: They make us feel our insignificance and powerlessness, and perhaps they turn us in thought towards the great Father for forgiveness and mercy.

DR. PAULUS: And yet man alone of all created things on this globe is gifted with the power of scientific research, even as he is with the faculty of discerning between good and evil. We can feel the deep significance of the psalmist's words: "Lord what is man that thou art mindful of him, and the son of man that thou visitest him? For thou hast made him a little lower than the angels; and hast crowned him with glory and honor. Thou makest him to have dominion over the works of thy hand; thou hast put all things under his feet."

THE PRESIDENT: Undoubtedly, man is a creature of mingled strength and weakness, and if he alone in the universe were capable of rising in thought and feeling above the finite, then were his position sad indeed. But if these mighty forces in nature are the works of an infinitely wise, holy, and gracious Being, the devout and humble-minded have every ground for hope and confidence in the tendency of things. As Scripture has been quoted I would again remind you of a passage from the Sacred Word, which always speaks eloquently to me, though it occurs in a sort of parenthesis (1 Cor. 8:5). "For though there be that are called God, whether in heaven or on earth; as there are gods many and lords many; yet to us there is one God, the Father, of whom are all things, and we unto Him; and one Lord, Jesus Christ, through whom are all things, and we unto Him."

MRS. VICTOR: I have reached almost the end of my notes and sketches, though I confess that I have not exhausted one-quarter of even the imperfect materials at my command. But there are many other noteworthy places for us to see, and too much time must not be given to any one of them. Here in these vast regions of mountain, forest, and desert, we seem to draw very close to the mysterious and awful powers of the universe. It is not all mere beauty in these mighty wilds, but beauty combined with awe-inspiring grandeur. How appropriate the thought of Milton, that much-neglected though always-praised poet, in the lines familiar to some of us from childhood:

THE FALLS OF SNAKE RIVER.

"These are thy glorious works, Parent of good,
Almighty, thine this universal frame,
Thus wondrous fair ; Thyself how wondrous then !
Unspeakable, who sitt'st above these heavens
To us invisible, or dimly seen
In these thy lowest works ; yet these declare
Thy goodness beyond thought, and power divine."

THE PRESIDENT : I think you have another sketch in your portfolio.

MRS. VICTOR : I had almost forgotten. Before we leave this upper Rocky Mountain region, or rather while we are upon the wing, I want you to accompany me for an aerial trip of a few minutes to a magnificent scene on the Snake River. The Shoshone Falls in Idaho are amphitheatrical in appearance. The Snake River here runs through a long and deep cañon formed by the action of its waters upon basaltic rocks. The falls are nearly a mile in width, and the adjacent rocks seven or eight hundred feet high. The descent of the main fall is about 400 feet, and below the cataract the sides of the cañon rise to a height of a thousand feet or more. Besides the Shoshone Falls there are other fine cataracts. The illustration gives a capital view of this weird spot.

CHAPTER X.

THE PLAINS AND PRAIRIES.

THE Fourth Conversational Tour of the J. U. T. C. was held at the house of Colonel Warlike.

The Minutes of the last meeting were read and confirmed.

Resolved, That the Secretary write out, at her convenience, and from her notes of the conversations, a full report of each meeting, and that the same be revised by the President, with a view to publication in a book form.

The conversation was begun by Colonel Warlike.

I am afraid, said the gallant Colonel, that I am not a very good hand at talking; but if the Club thinks that I can contribute in any way to its entertainment, I am willing to do my best.

Of course, you cannot expect that I can entertain you with many pictures of romantic scenery. The prairies and the plains of America do not present many striking objects for the artist's pencil; but in their vast extent they give one an idea of immensity from quite a different standpoint from the mountains. The prairies were at one time, not so long ago, the frontier lands. They lie between Ohio and Michigan, on the east, and the foot hills of the Rocky Mountains, but they do not, as you know, comprise the whole of this vast region. The western part of Ohio has some prairie lands, so has Michigan towards the south. Indiana, Illinois, Iowa, Wisconsin, the northern part of Missouri, Kansas and Nebraska, Dakota and Texas, are essentially prairie States; but the more easterly of these are well settled, and cultivated farms have taken the place of the wild lands once roamed by the buffalo and the savage Indian. Here is a view of what were once rolling prairie lands in Kansas. The scenery is diversified by trees, following the course of the river streams, but as you proceed farther west the trees disappear, except in the ravines, and on a few bluffs and ridges. Nothing but tall, rank, prairie grass, waving in the breeze, greets the eye of the traveler, during the summer months, for many a day's journey.

LILIAN: I understand that beautiful flowers grow on the prairie.

COLONEL WARLIKE: Oh yes; daisies, sunflowers, dandelions, and many others commonly to be met with in good dry grass lands, are here in abundance. Of course, you have all found out, if you did not know already, that the word prairie is French for meadow. American nomenclature is essentially cosmopolitan. The

VALLEY OF KANSAS RIVER.

different nations of the Old World send us not only their sons and daughters, but also portions of their vocabularies.

GILBERT: And, of course, we give an enlarged scope for every word we so appropriate. Our prairies are very large meadows, indeed, and must have been thought so by the early settlers.

ALBERT: What is the comparative elevation of prairie lands?

THE COLONEL: I must here refer to the President for information.

THE PRESIDENT: Their altitude varies, of course, very considerably. Lilian, you were copying some figures from The American Cyclopædia. Have you your notes with you?

LILIAN: Yes, papa. "Near Prairie du Chien, in West Wisconsin, the elevation of the prairies is about 400 feet above the Mississippi. At Cairo, in South Illinois, the upper surface is from 100 to 250 feet above the river, or 400 to 550 feet above the sea. In the central portion of the State, near the Illinois Central Railroad, the average elevation is from 650 feet to 750 feet above the sea, and near the northern border of the State this increases to 800 or 900 feet, and some of the highest swells of the prairie are 1,000 feet high. In South Wisconsin the more elevated portions of the prairie are about 1,100 feet above tide water. In Iowa the *plateau du coteau des prairies* of Nicollet, dividing the waters of the Mississippi from those of the Missouri, is from 1,400 to 1,500 feet above the sea." The article goes on to say, of the general character of the prairie surface: "On the head waters of the Illinois and Wabash, and south and west of Lake Michigan, the prairies are very level and smooth, and are termed flat. Those of other regions, where the surface is undulating, and broken by the depressions of the streams, are known as rolling prairies."

CLARA: Has any estimate been made of the extent of prairie lands in, say, square miles?

MR. GOLDUST: The Professor will correct me if I am wrong; but I have somewhere seen it stated that the prairies east of the Rocky Mountains embrace a territory of a thousand miles square, which would give a million square miles.

THE PRESIDENT: I am not aware that any serious attempt has been made as yet to measure the prairies, but the territory embraced in the geographical divisions of the continent generally designated as prairie land, and without taking into consideration the plains west of the Rocky Mountains, cannot be much less than mentioned by Mr. Goldust.

GRACE: Why are there no trees on the prairies?

THE COLONEL: I must again appeal to the President.

THE PRESIDENT: I do not know that the question has ever been quite satisfactorily answered. As a matter of fact some portions of prairie lands are by no means utterly destitute of trees. They are met with along some of the streams or bottoms, and occasionally elsewhere. In the settled parts of the prairies immense numbers of trees have been planted. In Iowa especially, which is a prairie State, great attention has been given to this branch of agriculture, and many millions of trees now exist and flourish. But, notwithstanding all this, the description of the prairies as treeless holds good in the main, and the culture of timber taxes the ingenuity and tries the patience of those who attempt it. Soil and climate, of course, are the two essential conditions one naturally looks to as determining the *flora* of any country. Some think that the soil, and some think that the climate is taxable with this peculiarity of the prairie, and probably both have something to do with it. In certain parts of England there are extensive tracts of downs where you see nothing in the shape of a tree for miles, and yet bordering the downs are luxuriant woods and leafy lanes. Take the County of Sussex, for example. The ranges of chalk hills to the south, known as the Sussex Downs, and on which the finest mutton in the world is fed, are treeless, and they are covered with a peculiarly sweet and nutritious grass and abundance of wild thyme. But Sussex, as a whole, is richly wooded. So that climate, here, would seem to have less to do with the subject than soil. Some think that the comparatively small rainfall over the prairie region is the chief cause of the absence of trees. The high ridges and peaks of the Rocky Mountains attract the clouds, leaving the plains comparatively rainless; again, the prevailing westerly winds carry the moisture rising from the gulf in an easterly direction, till it strikes the great Appalachian range of the Atlantic coast. We must, however, bear in mind the character of the soil of the prairies, including the surface soil and the underlying strata. Professor James Hall, a very high authority, thinks that this alone is sufficient to account for the prairies being treeless, the underlying rocks being mostly what is known in geology as shale, or consisting of slaty fragments. The surface soil is generally rich vegetable mould, from one or two feet deep, in the elevated parts, to one or two hundred feet deep in the rich bottom lands. Forest trees would seem to delight in a subsoil of a decided character, limestone rock, or well-defined clays or gravel. Mere richness of vegetable mould will not sustain oaks, elms, pine, or maple. Put both these causes together and we have probably about the truth of the matter.

AUNT HARRIET: If the Colonel will allow me, I will read a portion of a letter I

The Plains and Prairies.

have seen from a friend of mine who had the courage to settle with her husband and daughter in Nebraska. The letter says : " We are about eight miles west of the junction of the Sappa and Beaver creeks, on high, rolling prairie land. The atmosphere is remarkably clear. We have been able to get wood for firing and for building on the Beaver Creek, which is three miles north of us. On these prairies the regulation house is built of sod, and I can assure you is very warm and comfortable, as well as neat and good-looking, according to the taste of the inmates. They remind me of the houses of the farmers in some parts of Scotland—walls about three feet thick (though in Scotland the material is granite). The Indians hunted this region, but it is three years since the buffalo left, though there are plenty of tracks and bleached bones.

BUFFALO HUNTING.

"We have had one good sight of the mirage of the plains, when there appear to be splendid lakes, bordered by groves of trees, the waves rolling as with real water. I assure you the illusion is complete. The only trees here are along the courses of the rivers ; but as all available land is being rapidly taken, and a good deal of it is in timber claims, it will not be long before there will be groves on all hands. There are evidences, where the prairie has not been on fire for some time, of young timber."

THE PRESIDENT : That suggests a third cause to be considered in relation to the treeless condition of the prairies—prairie fires ; the long, dry grass of these regions being peculiarly susceptible to fires.

AUNT HARRIET : The letter from which I am reading goes on to say: "One Sunday, coming from church, we saw a prairie fire, spreading rapidly under pressure of a strong south wind. We felt safe, as there was a good ' fire-break ' all round our premises—that is, land ploughed, so that there is nothing for the fire to catch. But after dinner, to make doubly sure, we started another fire against the wind, and then took in the full grandeur of the scene all the evening, and went to bed with the waves of fire rolling all round, feeling far more secure than, under similar circumstances, we should have done in any city."

THE COLONEL: I am much obliged to you, and I am sure the Club is, for

SIOUX INDIANS.

furnishing so appropriate a contribution. And now, perhaps, you are expecting from me some of my personal experiences in the great prairie region.

JOHN: Pardon me for interrupting at this point, but I am curious about the distinction which is usually drawn between the plains and the prairies. What is the difference?

The Plains and Prairies.

THE COLONEL: In a military sense I think that the word plains as distinguished from prairies is that portion of the treeless, or nearly treeless, territory east of the Rocky Mountains more or less infested, until quite recently, by predatory Indians, whereas the prairies are more under cultivation, and free from Indian raids. The prairies lie to the east and the plains to the west of, say, the meridian of Leavenworth. The farther west you go from this line the more Indians you see, and the more wild and uninclosed the country; but, of course, the prairies are encroaching on the plains all the while.

MR. MERRIMAN: Civilization is "marching on."

THE COLONEL: Here are some groups of Indians—a party of four Sioux, some Utes and others. They are dressed in their best clothes, and do not look the terrible savages that they really are. Contrast their peaceful appearance with the Indian flourishing a scalp, and you will not wonder that they are the dread of frontiersmen and their families, and foemen worthy of the steel of the bravest and best of our soldiers. Fighting them is no mere pastime, I assure you.

We have heard of the Beaver Creek in Nebraska. It is now, I believe, the

SNAKE INDIANS FROM UTAH.

center of a district rapidly filling up; but the last and only time I passed through it was in the spring of 1869. I was then a junior officer in the Seventh Cavalry Regiment, of which General Custer was colonel, and our regiment formed part of General Hancock's expedition against the Cheyennes and Sioux, who were already on the warpath, and had committed many acts of spoliage and murder. Of course you will not expect me to give you the details of this expedition. It was my first experience with the savages. On one occasion I accompanied a squadron of my regiment as an escort of a train of wagons which our commanding officer had dispatched for supplies to Fort Wallace. We were to halt about midway down Beaver Creek, when our squadron was to divide, one company proceeding with the escort, and the other scouting up and down Beaver Creek till their return. I must, therefore, have been very near the spot from which the lady wrote the letter which has been read to us.

INDIANS.

ALBERT: Did you go with the wagons or remain in Beaver Creek?

THE COLONEL: It fell to my lot to remain at Beaver Creek, but on the second morning after the wagon train had left us we were greatly surprised by the arrival of another full squadron of cavalry bearing orders to our captain to join forces and proceed with all dispatch towards Fort Wallace, distant about fifty miles, until we met the returning wagon train, as it was suspected that the Indians were intending to attack and capture the train. Accordingly we started as soon as possible, and fortunately met the train about midway. The train, which was escorted by only about fifty soldiers, had been attacked by a force of several hundred Indians, and had had a sort of running fight for hours. Nothing but excellent tactics and judgment could have enabled our men to bear the brunt of such an attack, but they did, and killed several Indians, who were evidently hoping that our men would exhaust their ammunition, and then all would have been over with them. But in the very crisis of the battle the Indian scouts saw our troops, far away in the distance, galloping towards the scene, and they thought it prudent to retire for the time.

CYRIL: How did the Indians fight? Did they use rifles?

THE COLONEL: They had excellent rifles and fleet ponies as usual. Their plan was to circle round the train, firing from the sides of their ponies, at full gallop.

GRAND INDIAN "POW-WOW" WITH COMMISSIONERS.

They are wonderful adepts at this. But our men formed the wagons two abreast, with the horses between the columns, one trooper having charge of four horses. The other men on foot formed a guard round the moving wagons, and, as soon as any of the boys could get a shot at an Indian as he flew past, he fired. In this way the whole train kept moving along while defending itself.

JOHN: Were any of our men killed?

THE COLONEL: I think not in that engagement; but unfortunately a few days after, a lieutenant of cavalry and ten men, bearing despatches to our Colonel, were attacked by Indians, and after a desperate struggle were massacred to a man. We found the bodies brutally disfigured at Beaver Creek, and buried them.

BERTRAM: Pray go on, Colonel, with your adventures.

THE COLONEL: I must not do any such thing, or I should not know when to stop. I have here a few more illustrations, with which I hope you will allow me honorably to retire from my command. Here is a portrait of General Philip Sheridan, commander of the department of the Missouri during most of my term of service. I need not say that the General has had a most eventful and brilliant career as a soldier, and fully deserves the confidence and affection in which he is held by both the army and the nation at large. Here is a

INDIAN WITH SCALP.

THE WAPITI.

picture showing an interview or great council between Indian chiefs and a Commission from Washington. It is a good and characteristic sketch of one of these famous pow-wows.

AUNT HARRIET : I suppose that the Indian question will never seriously interest any but a small proportion of our people; otherwise we might even yet hope to see the Indian department creditably managed.

DR. PAULUS : I do not despair altogether of the future of the race, although there are many gloomy aspects of the question. The Church of Christ is grappling with the difficulty with more earnestness than ever. It is demonstrated, beyond doubt, that the Indian is capable of civilization, and I am glad to see that our government is encouraging and aiding the establishment of schools in the various tribes, with very gratifying results.

GENERAL SHERIDAN.

AUNT HARRIET : I hope it will not be long before Indian citizenship will be fully recognized.

MR. MERRIMAN : I believe that some of the wisest and most philanthropic men and women of our country are devoting their lives to the study of this great question, and it is devoutly to be hoped that the next decade or two will witness the dawn of a better state of things—a more enlightened and creditable administration of the department, and a greater tendency to peaceful pursuits on the part of the Indians.

THE COLONEL : I sincerely hope it may, but the Indian is a hard puzzle at best, though I admit that he has been used very badly. Miss Laura, you can give us some stanzas of Bryant's Soliloquy of an Indian at the burying place of his fathers.

LAURA : You mean that piece beginning :

"It is the spot I came to seek,
 My fathers' ancient burial place,
 Ere from these vales, ashamed and weak,
 Withdrew our wasted race."

It is too long to quote. I remember the verse—

" They waste us—ay—like April snow
  In the warm noon, we shrink away :
  And fast they follow, as we go
   Towards the setting day,
  Till they shall fill the land, and we
  Are driven into the western sea."

THE COLONEL : And now to change the topic, and before we leave the plains, let me show you a beautiful picture of the famous Wapiti deer (*Cervus Canadensis*), native of the Northern States, and found most abundantly on the upper Missouri and Yellowstone rivers. Sometimes it is called the elk, though improperly, as the true American Elk is what is called the moose (*Alces Americanus*), found in Maine, eastern Canada, Labrador, etc. The Wapiti is by far the nobler-looking animal of the two.

CHAPTER XI.

MOUNTAIN SCENERY IN PENNSYLVANIA.

HE next meeting of the J. U. T. C. was held at the house of Mr. John Smith, and after the transaction of the usual preliminary business, which occupied only a few minutes, the Conversational Tour of the evening was begun by the President calling upon Mr. John Smith first to lead the club through some of the mountain and river scenery of Pennsylvania.

JOHN (*reading from MS.*) : The Alleghany Mountains form a part of the great Appalachian chain, extending from the St. Lawrence River on the north, to Alabama in the south. The general direction of these mountains is from northeast to southwest, and they constitute the great easterly ridge of the northern continent.

Sometimes the whole range is generally spoken of by this title "Alleghany," the meaning of which is "endless"—Indian origin, of course. The name Appalachian was given to the range by the Spaniards under De Soto, who probably received it from the Indians, but I do not know the meaning of the word. The total length of the Appalachian range is about 1,300 miles, and its mean width about 100 miles. It comprises several extensive groups of mountains better known by their local names, such as the White Mountains of New Hampshire, the Adirondacks, the Catskills, the Highlands of the Hudson, the Cumberland, the Blue, the Black Mountains, etc., and the entire system of lateral hills and spurs of this eastern region of the continent.

The highest peaks of this range are in North Carolina and in New Hampshire. In the former State the Black Mountains rise to an elevation of between six and seven thousand feet above the sea ; and Mount Washington, in the White Mountains, has an altitude of 6,288 feet.

Geologically this mountain range is highly important. Granitic rocks containing veins of magnetic iron ore, limestone rocks, iron and coal of almost limitless ex-

VIEW ON THE JUNIATA RIVER.

tent, together with copper, lead, gold, silver and other mineral strata, abound. In some parts of the range rock salt exists in abundance, and in others salt is obtained by boring artesian wells, and evaporation.

The surface of these hills is clothed with noble forests, and the valleys are

THE JUNIATA.

watered by ever-flowing streams. The scenery is romantic, and in many parts full of grandeur.

This evening we will visit some of the most beautiful places along the Susque-

RAILWAY CUT NEAR HUNTINGDON.

hanna, the Juniata, and the Connemaugh Rivers, in Pennsylvania, in the heart of the Pennsylvania Alleghanies. These streams flow through a region of surpassing loveliness, well deserving the tribute paid to it by the late Thomas Buchanan Read :

> " Fair Pennsylvania! than thy midland vales,
> Lying 'twixt hills of green, and bound afar
> By billowy mountains rolling in the blue,
> No lovelier landscape meets the traveler's eye."

The Juniata—the names of all these rivers are Indian in their origin, and somewhat obscure as to their meaning—takes its rise at the foot of the Alleghany Mountains proper, and follows a winding course, in an easterly direction, for over a hundred miles to its junction with the Susquehanna, a few miles above Harrisburgh. Comparatively few persons are acquainted with this stream. In fact the whole of this region is worthy of far more attention than it receives from the tourist.

We will now imagine ourselves, if you please, at the romantic village of Huntingdon, 203 miles from Philadelphia, on the Harrisburgh and Pittsburgh division of the Pennsylvania railroad. This is the capital of the county of the same name—a county rich in agricultural produce, and in its stores of minerals, as yet hardly touched. Here we get many fine snatches of scenery.

Here is a very graphic picture showing a railway cut through one of the characteristic slaty ridges of the country, and giving a beautiful view of the valley and adjacent hills. Not far from this is a natural curiosity worth turning aside to see. A little tributary of the Juniata, called Arched Spring, flows for one mile under ground. Its entrance and its exit are shown in the two accompanying illustrations. I do not suppose that any one has been bold enough to follow this little stream through this one dark mile of its course, but you see that it comes at last back again to the sunlight, and sparkles and rejoices on its destined way. I think that we may draw a moral from this, though, in the dignified presence of our honorary members, I almost feel that it is presumptuous to suggest it.

THE PRESIDENT: We trust that the dignity of the honorary members will not be so great as to be unduly repressive upon the juniors. Pray let us have your moral.

Mountain Scenery in Pennsylvania. 113

JOHN: Simply this, that darkness, trial, and obscurity in a human life must not be confounded with failure. If this spring in the mountains never issued forth again as a brooklet to be seen and admired, its intrinsic value and, probably, its

INLET TO SINKING SPRING.

uses would be none the less important even in its rocky chambers than they are in the light of day.

KATE: Still I would rather have a little sunlight on my course than be all the time in darkness and obscurity.

JOHN: No doubt; and so would we all. And because that is so, we too readily despond or misjudge if for a time the sunlight is withdrawn from us, or from our neighbor.

DR. PAULUS: " He that goeth forth and weepeth, bearing precious seed, shall

OUTLET TO THE SINKING SPRING.

doubtless come again with rejoicing, bringing his sheaves with him." Thank you for your moral, John.

AUNT HARRIET: I am reminded of Longfellow's poem, "The Two Rivers":

> " O River of yesterday, with current swift,
> Through chasms descending, and soon lost to sight,
> I do not care to follow in their flight,
> The faded leaves, that on thy bosom drift !

LEWISTOWN NARROWS.

O River of to-morrow, I uplift
Mine eyes and thee I follow,——
*   *   *   sure to meet the sun,
And confident that what the future yields
Will be the right, unless myself be wrong."

JOHN: We will now descend the river for a few miles till we come to Lewistown. All around us as we journey are charming and picturesque glens, vales, and water courses.

Here the train passes through a narrow defile or gorge called Lewistown Narrows, suggestive, though on a less magnificent scale, of the cañons of the West.

From this point we will retrace our steps and travel westward for a few score miles, taking an air-line, or a bee-line, if you please, to Altoona, a large city of over 20,000 inhabitants, built up within the past thirty years as the site of the machine shops of the Pennsylvania railroad. This city lies at the easterly foot of the Alleghanies proper, and the surrounding scenery is grand and beautiful beyond expression. The railroad here ascends by a very steep grade towards the west, requiring two engines, whereas trains coming east run down eleven miles without one single particle of steam force—a long inclined plane. At the top of the mountain there is a tunnel about three-quarters of a mile long, after which the line descends the western slope of the Alleghanies towards the Ohio Valley, and so on to Chicago and the West. Two or three miles west of the tunnel, and on the dividing ridge of the mountains, is the village of Cresson, celebrated for its mineral waters and for its cool, breezy atmosphere during the summer. It is a delightful place for a summer's holiday. And now, if you please, we will take a glimpse of the scenery in this locality, and farther on in the region of the Connemaugh and Kiskiminetas.

GRACE: What delightful Indian names! I am so glad they have not changed them into prosaic modern names.

JOHN: What do you say then to the title of this picture, "Kettle-Run, Altoona?"

It is a sketch of a lovely and romantic forest glade, but Altoona sounds to me somewhat Dutch-like, and as for Kettle-Run, there is a decidedly Yankee notion in that name, or I am very much mistaken.

KETTLE-RUN, ALTOONA.

ALBERT: I suppose Kettle-Run is the name of the brook.

JOHN: Yes, and so christened from a remarkable hollow surrounded by hills, and said to resemble a kettle, through which it flows. There is a curious State law which forbids the cutting of timber along this stream, and the consequence is that its banks are densely wooded, and the stream itself a good deal obstructed by falling trees and moss-grown logs and boulders.

Our next view is a very fine one of the great "Horseshoe Bend" in the railroad, between, I think, Altoona and Cresson. A great many engineering difficulties had, of course, to be overcome in the construction of this mountain line. Before this road was built the old Portage railroad used to convey the trains by sections up and down inclined planes, but now there is no break in the journey, although at times during the descent, on either side, the traveler cannot avoid a feeling of apprehension, though fortunately accidents hereabouts are extremely rare, owing to the great precautions observed.

BERTRAM: Is this the old regular beaten track from east to west?

JOHN: I believe it was the direct road taken from the earliest times by the immigrants to Ohio; that is to say, the route lay along the banks of the Juniata, and away over the Alleghanies at this point. The whole of this region and far out beyond, among the hills and valleys of Pennsylvania, is peopled largely by the Dutch and their descendants—a thrifty, old-time race, keeping their ancestral faith and customs, and not permitting the outside world, by reason of the introduction of the steam railroad into their hills and valleys, to rob them of their heritage, or to seduce them with its vanities.

LAURA: How came it that Pennsylvania has so many people of German and Dutch descent in it? Penn was an Englishman, at any rate.

JOHN: I think I must refer to our President for an explanation of that important fact.

THE PRESIDENT: I think it largely due to the fame which this State early acquired for good government and wise toleration of religious preferences. Penn himself was a man of exceeding nobleness and liberality of view. He had the good fortune to be strongly backed by the English government, though in many respects he was in character the very antipode of the Stuart kings. The colony soon acquired a reputation for stability, which, combined with the material advantages of

KITTANNING POINT, "HORSE SHOE BEND."

soil and climate it offered to the settler, and the policy of William Penn to welcome good men without respect to race or religion, drew towards it the attention of the European nations in an especial manner. The Dutch, however, were really on the ground before Penn, and the Swedes even before them; so that when Penn came upon the scene he found a country already in part settled; at least along the course of the Delaware, for a considerable distance. In the first half of the last century a strong German Protestant emigration set in, meeting another steady stream of Scotch and Scotch-Irish Presbyterians, and giving a decided tone to the population of the State.

MR. GOLDUST : That old Portage Road of which mention has been made is an interesting relic. I remember traveling over it in 1835. It was a connecting link, thirty-five miles long, between Johnstown on the western side of the Alleghanies, and Hollidaysburg on their eastern slopes. From Hollidaysburg there was a canal to Philadelphia, and from Johnstown there was a canal to Pittsburg. The first scheme to make this important link between east and west was by means of a canal with locks, but the difficulty and expense seemed insuperable. Then this old Portage road was built at a cost of nearly two million dollars. All the bridges were of stone ; the rails were imported from England ; and the whole was a solid and durable affair.

BERTRAM : Was it a steam road ?

MR. GOLDUST : The inclined planes were worked by stationary engines, and the level portions of the road by horses at first, but afterwards by locomotives. There was a new Portage road built in 1856 without any inclined planes, and with two or three long tunnels; but even this was at last abandoned, or sold to the Pennsylvania Railroad Company, who laid out and constructed the present track. Both of these Portage roads are now in ruins ; the rails have been removed, and much of the road beds has been broken away by torrents, or obstructed by fallen trees. The tunnels are also unused.

At this stage travel for this evening was suspended, and the proceedings became informal.

CHAPTER XII.

THE SUSQUEHANNA AND DELAWARE RIVERS.

HE sixth evening was spent at the house of Mr. Goldust, and after the transaction of the usual routine business, Miss Laura Smith was invited to lead the club in a Conversational Tour through portions of the Susquehanna and Delaware Valleys.

LAURA (reading from notes): The river Susquehanna, from the Indian, signifying "Crooked River," is a noble stream, four hundred miles in length, taking its rise from Otsego lake, New York, and emptying itself, after a very tortuous course, through highly picturesque scenery, into the Chesapeake Bay, at Havre de Grace. Lake Otsego, with its magnificent hemlock trees, which give quite a character to its scenery, is classic region in American literature, the novelist J. Fennimore Cooper having made it the scene of many of his powerful stories.

Our party went to Otsego Lake from Albany by the Albany and Susquehanna Railroad. We stopped at Cooperstown, and made that village our head-quarters. The village is close to the lake on the south. The lake is about 1,200 feet above the sea, a beautiful sheet of water, eight or nine miles long, by about a mile broad, and set in a cluster of hills. Cooper has made the region very famous, and indeed it is a very charming place, and we enjoyed many a delightful sail upon its waters.

THE PRESIDENT : You have probably looked up some facts about Cooper. As he is so closely associated with this region we ought to know something about him.

LAURA : Yes, I find that James Fennimore Cooper was the son of the founder of Cooperstown. His father owned a good deal of the land in this region, which was then (1790) on the frontier. Cooper was only a few months old when his father moved from Burlington, N. J., to Otsego Lake, and his boyhood was spent in this romantic and Indian-trodden region. At sixteen years old he entered the navy and served six years. He married in 1811, resigned his commission as lieutenant, and took up his residence at Mamaroneck, N. Y., where he wrote some of his earlier publications. The first work of his which attracted general attention was the "Spy," founded on American Revolutionary incidents; then came "The Pilot," "The Last of the Mohicans," and other volumes. He went to Europe in 1827, lived there six years, and wrote several works. On his return, his writings took a satirical bias, and he was much criticised by the American press for showing up the peculiarities of his countrymen. He settled down into a regular course of literary work at Cooperstown, and died of dropsy in 1851.

THE PRESIDENT: What do you consider the chief characteristics of Cooper as an author.

LAURA: I am hardly qualified to sit as a critic, but what little I have read of Cooper gives me the impression of a wonderfully imaginative faculty, in which the results of close and vivid observation serve as the groundwork, and give a living interest to his works hardly second to that of Sir Walter Scott.

MR. GOLDUST: I have never read a line of Cooper, and always supposed that his books were very trashy productions.

THE PRESIDENT: That depends upon the reader to a great extent; in reading fiction a great deal of mental winnowing has to be done, and it is this which makes it undesirable to become a great novel reader—the majority of people read for mere excitement, or to kill time, and forget what is really valuable as soon as it is read.

LAURA: Cooperstown was the home of the novelist after his return from Europe, and the neighborhood is full of interest on his account.

In its course to the Atlantic the Susquehanna passes through a rich and beautiful country, receiving many tributaries, large and small, in its course. Passing into Pennsylvania, it waters the charming and famed Vale of Wyoming, where we again tread upon classic, even if we may not say, hallowed ground.

You are aware that this little valley—some twenty miles long by about three broad, and exceedingly lovely and peaceful in aspect, nestling between bold and rugged hills—was the scene of a fearful massacre during the war of Independence, and has been immortalized by the poet Campbell in his poem, Gertrude of Wyoming. The date of the massacre was July 3d, 1778. This district was then pretty well settled by an industrious, farming people. Sir Henry Clinton was commander of the British forces at Philadelphia, and had earned anything but an honorable name as a soldier by the countenance he gave to marauding and robbery in the name of warfare. Most of the men of Luzerne county, in which Wyoming is situated, were away in Washington's army, when an infamous man, an American tory named Major Butler, planned a raid from New York State into Pennsylvania, and suddenly appeared on the banks of the Susquehanna near Wilkesbarre with six-

BANKS OF THE SUSQUEHANNA.

teen hundred men, half Indians, and half Canadians and British. The inhabitants gathered together, and, fortifying an old fort, defended themselves as best they could, but at length capitulated, on Butler's assurance that their lives would be spared. The instant they surrendered the massacre began, and hundreds of men, women, and children were slaughtered. Then the raiders separated into companies, and pillaged the whole country, driving the few surviving people into the mountains and swamps.

I do not propose to take the Club any farther along the course of this river. At Sunbury it receives the waters of its principal tributary, the west branch of the Susquehanna, itself a goodly stream 200 miles in length. Afterwards it receives the Juniata ; and thence flows into Chesapeake Bay.

We now turn to some points of interest on the Delaware and Schuylkill Rivers.

The Delaware offers many attractions to the landscape-loving tourist, besides being a river of great historic renown in the history of this country. Like its sister the Susquehanna, it rises in New York State, its beginning being the union of two little streams flowing from the Catskill Mountains. For about seventy miles of its course it forms the boundary between New York and Pennsylvania, and afterwards it divides Pennsylvania from New Jersey.

Dr. Paulus : What is the origin of the name?

Laura : From the first governor of Virginia, Lord De La Ware, I believe.

Gilbert : Is there not an Indian tribe of the same name ?

Laura : Certainly—the Renappi, as they called themselves, but they were christened Delawares by the English because their home was on the banks of our river.

The Delaware Water Gap, at the northern extremity of Northampton County, and on the line of the Delaware, Lackawanna, and Western Railroad, is a defile in the Kittatinny or Blue Mountains, with nearly perpendicular rocks 1,200 to 1,600 feet high on either side. The gorge is about two miles long, and at the southeast end the passage is so narrow that the river and the railroad have, so to speak, to crowd close together to get through.

Just above the gap at the north end is a valley called Minnisink—Indian, "whence the waters are gone." A great lake once had its waters here, and where it has gone to is the mystery which has come down to us in its Indian tradition and name.

This is a lovely spot and is much visited. Of the two mountain barriers, that on the New Jersey side has been named Tammany, after an Indian chief ; and I suppose that this is the origin of the name assumed by a political party in New York city. The other side is named Mt. Minsi, also an Indian name I suppose.

Mr. Merriman : The illustration shows only one side of the gap—which is it ?

VIEW OF A SPUR OF THE BLUE MOUNTAINS, DELAWARE WATER GAP, NEW JERSEY.

LAURA : The New Jersey, or east side—Mount Tammany. It rises up, steep and bare, with a frowning, ominous outline. On its summit is a beautiful little lake, a mile across. Of course the views are very broad and beautiful from both hills, and from many points. And, by the way, there is a "lovers' leap" from one of the promontories of Mt. Minsi, and an Indian legend, which I suppose I may give.

MR. MERRIMAN : Let us hear it, by all means.

LAURA : Be it known that when the Dutch made their first settlements on the Delaware River, calling the place New Netherlands, in the beginning of the seventeenth century, a certain Indian maiden named Winona, daughter of the mighty chief Wissonoming, fell in love with young Hendrick Van Allen, an officer in one of the Dutch expeditions. The young man returned her affection, but unfortunately the expedition was not successful, and he was ordered home to Holland. For some time he wavered between the claims of love and of his country, but finally decided in favor of the latter. On informing the poor Indian girl of his decision, she sprang from his side and flung herself over the precipice.

KATE : I think he was decidedly mean.

LAURA : Although I have only shown you one illustration of the gap, I would have you understand that the vicinity is full of romantic spots, hills, vales, and glens, and a summer may be spent very delightfully in this region.

Passing by the many picturesque spots in the upper Delaware, which tempt us to linger, we will now make a rapid stride to the Schuylkill River.

THE PRESIDENT : I think it would interest the club to be reminded of some of the historic attractions of the Delaware River, to which you alluded a few minutes ago.

LAURA : I had almost forgotten. I have already spoken of the early Dutch settlements. Besides this there were very early settlements from Sweden, and a portion of country west of the river was named New Sweden. Eventually all came into possession of the English, and, Penn having obtained a grant of Pennsylvania from Charles II., an adjustment of the boundaries had to be made, and for a time what is now the State of Delaware was part of Pennsylvania. It seceded in 1691 with the reluctant consent of Penn.

GILBERT : Why did it secede?

LAURA : I have not read enough of history to give the full reason, but it was dissatisfied with certain acts of the State Assembly and preferred to legislate upon its own affairs. It was one of the most peaceful acts of secession which the world ever witnessed. It was fortunate for the settlers in the lower counties, as they were termed, that they had to deal with so peace-loving and honorable a governor as Wm. Penn, and that his spirit had been caught by the populations of the whole State. Little Delaware was allowed to depart in peace, and grew up to be a thriving community. Are you tired of history?

THE COLONEL : By no means ; we cannot do better than make these beautiful views assist our memories as to the events with which they are more or less closely connected.

LAURA : It was upon the banks of the Delaware, that Penn held his first conference with the Indian chiefs. The land between the Delaware and Schuylkill rivers, where Philadelphia now stands, was owned by three Swedes. Penn purchased the interest of the owners and laid it out for a city, giving names to some of the streets, such as Chestnut, Walnut, etc., which they hold to this day.

In the war of Independence this river was the scene of many thrilling incidents, which cannot all be recounted this evening. You have all seen the picture of Washington crossing the Delaware on his march to Trenton. He had been chased with his small army through New Jersey by Cornwallis, and had had to cross the river as a fugitive. This was at the very darkest hour of American history, when the hearts of the tories were rejoicing at the prospect of Washington's utter defeat. But Washington rallied and determined on recrossing the river and recapturing Trenton. On the night of Christmas, 1776, he accomplished this feat, in the piercing winter cold, the wind cutting like knives, and the twenty-five hundred faithful soldiers of that little army poorly clad, weary, and faint with fasting. They found, as they expected, that the Hessian troops at Trenton were asleep or drunk after their Chrismas carousals. This victory was the dawn of better things for America, and the Delaware will always be associated with this crisis in her affairs.

You are aware also that the mouth of the Delaware, below its junction with the Schuylkill, was the scene of important engagements in October, 1776, between the British ships and the American forts, and that Philadelphia was for some time the head-quarters of British forces. You have also heard of the battle of Germantown ; but this brings me to the end of my stock of reminiscences for the present.

CHAPTER XIII.

NIAGARA FALLS.

THE seventh Conversational Tour of the series was undertaken at the house of Mr. Victor, and was commenced (after the usual introductory business had been transacted) by Aunt Harriet, who was invited to conduct the club to Niagara Falls.

AUNT HARRIET: I do not know but that I have the most difficult task of any, for I suppose every member of this club has seen "The Falls," and then they have been so often described that it is well nigh impossible to present them in any novel light. But I shall invite you all to take a liberal share of responsibility this evening, while I try to be as matter of fact and unconventional as possible under the circumstances.

You are aware that that portion of the St. Lawrence stream which lies between Lake Erie and Lake Ontario is called Niagara River, or river of "the thundering waters." This river intersects an isthmus thirty-three miles and a half long, dividing the lakes. As the level of Ontario is 334 feet lower than that of Erie, it is evident that the Niagara River must descend very rapidly. This descent is, at the present time, classified in three divisions: first, the rapids, which accomplish 52 feet in less than a mile; second, the Falls themselves, which have a depth of about 160 feet; and third, the river below the falls, which descends about 110 feet or more, leaving about twelve or fourteen feet for the descent of the river between the outlet of Erie and the beginning of the rapids.

The pouring forth of an immense body of water, the outcome of four mighty lakes, draining half a continent, through this channel into the abyss of Ontario, gives an effect which, for grandeur and a sense of irresistible power, has no parallel on the face of the earth. We can hardly conceive of the force involved in this plunge over the rocks of, say, one hundred millions of tons of water every hour, year after year, century after century. The mind cannot at once grasp the thought, and it is only after one has sat some time in silence within sight and

FALLS OF NIAGARA, WEST SIDE.

sound of the cataract that its inexpressible majesty dominates the senses, and brings one helplessly beneath its spell.

LILIAN : I think I felt this most one afternoon when I clambered about half way down the steep on the Canadian side, a few hundred yards from the Falls, and sat there alone among the rocks for—I do not know how long. I was completely fascinated. It seemed as though I were no longer of this world at all.

CLARA : And then the indescribable melody of these mighty waters! Thundering is in one sense a very appropriate word, especially to convey the idea one gets of Niagara *at first*, or at some distance ; but as you listen, and listen, the most glorious harmony grows out of all this tumult.

BERTRAM : That reminds me of an article in a recent number of the *Century*, in which the writer, Mr. Eugene Thayer, says, in effect, that he never heard the *roar* of Niagara, but only and always a perfectly constructed and most exquisite harmony of musical sounds; and he elaborates this thought out very ingeniously, and as I think very truthfully.

DR. PAULUS : You remind me of Thomson's Hymn on the Seasons :

" His praise, ye brooks attune—ye trembling rills ;
And let me catch it, as I muse along.
Ye headlong torrents, rapid and profound,
* * *
Sound His stupendous praise."

THE PRESIDENT : It seems more consistent, certainly, to associate the idea of praise with that of harmony than with a discordant roar. The poets in all ages have given to inanimate nature this quality of finding expression in musical sounds.

AUNT HARRIET : Here is a view of the Falls from the Canada side, which will help us, I think, to understand Lilian's feelings in her solitary musings.

THE COLONEL : It looks as though there must be a gradual process of crumbling away going on in the rock formations. What is your idea on that point, Professor ?

THE PRESIDENT : There can be no reasonable doubt that the Falls are destined to undergo very great and perhaps sudden changes in the future, as they undoubtedly have in the past. The geological formation is highly favorable to change.

We have not the old granitic and basaltic rocks of the Yellowstone, and, on the other hand, we have an almost immeasurably greater volume of water—less resisting power and more force.

MR. GOLDUST : What is the geological character of the bed of Niagara ?

THE PRESIDENT : It is not of a uniform character. Professor Hall, the geologist, describes the bed of the Falls as a limestone rock resting on a shaly deposit, which gradually wears away, causing the upper rock, from time to time, to crumble into the abyss. Two miles farther up, towards Erie, the limestone gives place to shales and marls of the Onondaga Salt group, which of course would offer a very slight resistance to such a force. It may be thousands of years, however, before the water wears through these two miles of limestone.

THE COLONEL : If I understand you it is not the actual wear of the limestone rock so much as the undermining process in the softer shales which underlie it, that is mainly instrumental in effecting these changes in the river bed.

THE VERTICAL STAIRS.

THE PRESIDENT : Exactly. You see this in this picture of the vertical stairs, and also in the Cave of the Winds. It becomes very evident to the senses that the lower portion of the rock is hollowing in, so to speak, and it is but a question of time for the weight of the superincumbent mass to cause it to yield, a portion at a time probably.

THE AMERICAN FALL.

CLARA: I shall be afraid to go again into the Cave of the Winds.

THE PRESIDENT: The contingency is sufficiently remote to remove the idea of any great peril.

AUNT HARRIET: It is only within the present century that careful observations have been made of the channel, and yet, since then, various facts have been established. In 1818, large portions were detached from the crust of the American Fall, and in 1828 the same thing occurred with the Horse-Shoe Fall. Table Rock has entirely disappeared, within, I think, twenty years. The view of the American Fall shows an accumulation of detritus and rock at the foot, of which visitors are availing themselves. Further, it is said that the rate of retrogression of the falls is about a foot a year, and that this fact is established by observations made within the past forty years.

The descent from the Canadian side close to the Fall is either

THE HORSE-SHOE FALLS.

from the tower, or by steps cut in the rock. A fee is charged in either case, for as yet the property on both sides of the river is in private hands. Efforts have been made by both the Canadian and the American government to purchase these private rights, but up to the present time these efforts have not been successful, and the visitor is met at every turn by a request for money. There is nothing to do but to submit to these exactions with all the grace and patience possible, or to be content with such general views as one can get.

I think I have here the most striking picture of the Horse-Shoe Falls I remem-

OLD SUSPENSION BRIDGE, NIAGARA FALLS.

ber to have seen. Of course the effect is considerably heightened by the concealment of the river by the clouds of spray and vapor, but the sublimity of the scene is very faithfully depicted.

In visiting the Falls from the American side one usually first crosses the bridge to Goat Island, which divides the American from the Center Fall. From this bridge you get a grand view of the Rapids, and you also see a little island that has been made memorable by the rescue from it of a workman who fell into the stream while working on the bridge. Fortunately he was borne against this island and was taken off, at great risk to his rescuer. From Goat Island we proceed by a short foot-bridge to Luna Island and thence by the Biddles stairs to the Cave of the Winds, which is immediately below the Center Fall. But I must not attempt to lead you through all the sights. I ought to say that the width of the American Fall is a thousand feet, and that of the Horse-Shoe Fall two thousand two hundred feet, while the depth of water *over* the Fall is *at least* twenty feet.

GILBERT: How did they find that out?

AUNT HARRIET: By sending a large disused ship, drawing over eighteen feet,

THE WHIRLPOOL.

adrift over the Falls. She cleared the rocks without touching, and plunged over.

You have, of course, crossed the river at the foot of the Falls in the boat, and also walked over the Suspension Bridge, which, with its towers, one on either side of the gorge, is worth visiting for the excellent views they offer both of the Falls and the surrounding scenery. Another good point is the Railroad Suspension Bridge, which has also a carriage and a foot way, and is two miles below the cataract. A mile farther down the river is the famous whirlpool, preceded by the whirlpool rapids.

Turning now from the physical features of these scenes, of which I have not even mentioned one half that are striking, I must refer briefly to some of the historical characteristics of this vicinity.

During the war of 1812 this was a great battle ground. At Queenston, about seven miles from the Falls on the Canada side, and directly opposite Lewiston, stands a monument to General Brock, who fell there in an engagement between the American and British forces on October 11, 1812. The Canadians point to this monument with a great deal of pride, as it not only represents the deeds of a brave soldier, but signalizes the repulse of the first and only serious invasion of Canadian soil since its unification under the British Crown.

CYRIL: Why do you say serious?

AUNT HARRIET: Because I can hardly dignify the Fenian invasion of 1866 as serious, although in one sense it was so, undoubtedly. It was so utterly chimerical, and withal so futile, that it brought the cause which it was intended to serve into ridicule, though it succeeded in arousing a thoroughly patriotic and military spirit among the Canadians.

MR. MERRIMAN: It was a serious scare for the Canadians too. I was in Toronto at the time of the Fenian invasion on business, and the excitement there was very great. The volunteers met and engaged the Fenian force about ten miles from Fort Erie, on the Welland Canal, at a spot called Limeridge, and the result was not very decisive on either side. The Canadians were inexperienced soldiers, not very well officered, and the Fenians were certainly no better in that respect. Several were killed on both sides, and O'Neil, the Fenian leader, thought it prudent to make his way across the frontier during the following night. Meanwhile the Fenians had also planned an elaborate attack on Prescott, with the view of marching on to Ottawa the seat of the Dominion government, but by this time the American government were aroused to a sense of duty, and nipped the enterprise in the bud. For a long time afterwards Canada was intensely excited over this impudent attack.

ALBERT: Is not Lundy's Lane in the vicinity of Niagara?

AUNT HARRIET: Yes, and that also was the scene of an engagement between the American and British forces on July 25th, 1814. Lundy's Lane is a very short distance from the Falls. On this occasion both sides lost heavily, and both claimed the victory, but the British held possession of the field.

KATE: I am no doubt very ignorant about these matters, but I feel very much inclined to ask, with little Peterkin or his sister—I forget which—

"Now tell us all about the war
And what they killed each other for."

AUNT HARRIET: I would like to appeal to our friend John Smith for information.

JOHN: You compliment me greatly, and I can only say that in my judgment, based upon a very moderate amount of historical reading, the war of 1812 grew out of the high-handed way in which the British administration dealt with American interests, commercial and otherwise, towards the close of the Napoleon-French war, when Great Britain was virtually mistress of the seas—fanned as this complaint undoubtedly was by a preponderance of sympathy with France in America, and probably by a desire of the Democratic party, then in power in America, to annex Canada to the United States. America had been bullied a good deal by Great Britain, and she was spirited enough to resent the insults shown her, and to retaliate in kind.

DR. PAULUS: It is strange how soon Christian nations will drift into war with each other for causes which, in the hands of half a dozen impartial and intelligent men, could be adjusted, perhaps, in a single day.

AUNT HARRIET: I am very much of the opinion of the Prussian barber about whom Dr. Russell in "Hesperothen" tells us, who, in reply to a question which seemed to throw a doubt upon his patriotism, said that in his opinion "fighting was nonsense"—very disastrous nonsense, no doubt, but still without sense or reason to justify it.

THE PRESIDENT: What do you say to that, Colonel?

THE COLONEL: I quite agree with Miss Victor in the main; but the business of the soldier is to fight whenever his country orders him to do so, and not to go into any reasons for or against.

AUNT HARRIET: I think we are getting a little wide of our subject, and as we have another and a longer journey to take this evening, I think we must bid farewell to Niagara with all its associations, its beauty, and its sublimity.

THE PRESIDENT: It will interest us, however, if you can furnish us with any more historical points. They contribute largely to the value and the delight of our excursions.

AUNT HARRIET: Let me see. A little west of Lundy's Lane is Chippewa Creek, where, on the 5th of July, 1814, a severe battle was fought between the Americans and the British. This time it was the British who got the worst of it, being driven into their intrenchments. This was about three weeks before the battle of Lundy's Lane. It is but fair to state that the struggle was a very severe one, and that before the winter the Americans thought it prudent to retire across the river to Buffalo.

On the south side of the river the towns of Lewiston and of Niagara were both scenes of warlike operations. Lewiston was captured and burnt by the British, together with Youngstown and Manchester, in the campaign of 1813; while Newark, a Canadian town near Fort George, was burnt by the American General McClure just before these events.

In fact, the whole Niagara isthmus was terribly harassed during this war of 1812–1814. The Indians fought chiefly on the British side, and were valuable and powerful allies.

GILBERT: How did it all end?

AUNT HARRIET: As far as I can understand, both nations grew heartily sick and tired of the war. Commissioners met at Ghent in Belgium in 1814, and, after spending some months in negotiations, signed a treaty of peace. In this treaty not a word was said about the original causes of offense, and its main provisions related simply to some petty matters about boundary lines.

THE PRESIDENT: The war was a disgrace all round. It inflicted untold injuries upon this country, from which our people long suffered in many ways. At the same time it taught England a wholesome lesson. The only parties that came out of the war with real credit were the Canadians, who, with the assistance of the mother country, kept their territory inviolate, and even profited by the war. England paid her own bills, and also in the main those of Canada.

DR. PAULUS: Let us hope that the good sense of all parties will prevent any such misunderstanding in the future, or that, at any rate, should causes of offense arise, they may be settled by honorable conference or arbitration without bloodshed.

CHAPTER XIV.

LAKE SUPERIOR.

ALBERT: Away, if you please, up to the northern boundary of the United States, the south coast line of Lake Superior. If we were about to make the tour of the upper lakes, we should probably start from Buffalo, and occupy two weeks going and returning; but on this occasion I invite you to undertake a portion only of this tour.

We can take an aerial flight across the province of Ontario in Canada, over a portion of Lake Huron, leaving the great Georgian Bay and Manitoulin Island to our right, and meet the steamer in the St. Mary River, the strait, or stream (it is sixty-two miles long), connecting Lakes Superior and Huron. We avoid the rapids by going through the ship canal, and soon find ourselves on the bosom of this majestic inland sea—the largest body of fresh water in the world. Shall I give the dimensions?

KATE: Certainly.

ALBERT: Lake Superior is 360 miles long, with an average width of eighty-five miles. It has a shore line of 1,500 miles, and an area of 32,000 square miles. It drains a territory of at least 100,000 square miles, and its bottom is 200 feet lower than the level of the ocean. Its depth is about 800 feet in the deepest portions. These, of course, are guide-book facts; but they are necessary to know, if we would have a fair idea of our subject.

The scenery around this lake is rocky and picturesque, and there are not a few associations connected with it which make it very interesting to the tourist.

I have three views only for your inspection, but they are of scenes which, on more than one account, are peculiarly memorable. They show us portions of what are known as the Pictured Rocks. These rocks extend for about five miles along the southern shore at the widest part of the lake, and derive their name from the different colors distributed in regular strata or lines upon their seaward surface. These bands of brilliant color are produced by the percolation of water through the porous sandstone. The water is impregnated with iron and copper, and on its exposure to the air conveys a tone or tint to the cliff. The rocks themselves are from one to three hundred feet high, and have been buffeted and beaten by the action of the winds and waves into all manner of grotesque and fantastic shapes. They descend precipitously into the water, with little or no intervening beach, so that to inspect them thoroughly one has to land and take a sail or row boat.

Here we have a view of Grand Chapel rocks, which I see the artist has given us with all the surroundings of a thunder-storm. It looks a weird and awful place. The roof of the chapel is arched and supported by beautiful columns, and a broken column inside has the appearance of a pulpit or altar. The roof is crowned with trees and shrubs.

Speaking of thunder-storms I ought to say that Lake Superior is very subject to them, and indeed to storms of all kinds, and that their effect is plainly visible along its coasts and headlands. The imagination of the Indians peopled this region with all kinds of evil spirits, and made it the scene of violent conflicts. Some of the Indian traditions and legends have been gathered skillfully together by Longfellow in "The Song of Hiawatha," of which we may perhaps hear something by and by from another member of this club.

MR. GOLDUST: It is creditable to the person who invented the names for these places that so respectable and pious a title has been selected for the rock we have just been looking at. It is a decided change for the better from the Satanic or Titanic nomenclature one expects to find in such regions as these.

MR. MERRIMAN: We must remember that the region of Lake Superior was early visited by Christian missionaries of the Catholic persuasion, and probably the circumstance you notice may be due to their early presence on the field. I am not a Catholic, but I think there is much to admire, and even to revere, in the missions of the Jesuit Fathers to the North American Indians. We have, among the many islands of this lake, The Apostles, The St. Ignace, and Pio (or Pius) islands.

ALBERT: My second view is of a picturesque cascade a little to the west of the Chapel. It is a small affair compared with some cataracts we have lately vis-

"GRAND CHAPEL" ROCKS.

ited, but it is a pleasant object to see and hear in these watery wilds, and we may do worse than linger for a while within sound of its ceaseless flow.

The third view is of what is known as the Great Cave—a very peculiar and striking object. It is a huge rectangular mass projecting some distance from the line of the cliffs. On the lake side there is a beautiful archway, a hundred and fifty feet high, and on the other two sides there are small openings. These lead to an interior apartment, irregular, and strewn with *débris*, and with smaller caverns, or recesses in the walls. The whole interior is moss-grown. The waves of the lake drive into this cavern during storms with mighty force, working constant changes.

CASCADE NEAR CHAPEL ROCKS.

There are other natural features of this group of rocks which are worth describing, but I shall not now stop to do so, as our visit must be brief. Do not forget, if you sail among these rocks again, to look out for the Empress of the Lake—a profile not noticeable by day, but which comes out very clearly by moonlight. And now, as I know that my aunt has been quietly reading Longfellow for the last two or three days, I would beg of her to give us some idea of those Indian legends to which I referred a few minutes ago.

AUNT HARRIET: Longfellow's poem of Hiawatha is full of them, and some refer to this region. You have all, however, read the poem, doubtless.

MR. GOLDUST: I have not.

Lake Superior. 143

LAURA: I tried to read it, but could not make head or tail out of it, it seemed so absurd. I suppose I must be very stupid.

GRACE: I just remember that there is a love story in it between Hiawatha and

THE GREAT CAVE.

Minnehaha, or Laughing Water, and that they lived very happily together, until Minnehaha died one winter of fever or famine, or something.

AUNT HARRIET: If you read the introduction to the poem you will be tempted to read it through, though some of it may seem at first a tissue of absurdity.

> Ye whose hearts are fresh and simple,
> Who have faith in God and Nature;
> Who believe that in all ages
> Every human heart is human;
> That in even savage bosoms
> There are longings, yearnings, strivings,
> For the good they comprehend not;
> That the feeblest hands, and helpless,
> Groping blindly in the darkness,
> Touch God's right hand in that darkness,
> And are lifted up and strengthened :—
> Listen :

DR. PAULUS: "In every nation, he that feareth God and worketh righteousness is accepted of him."

THE PRESIDENT: Perhaps the chief merit of this poem is the studious fidelity to Indian tradition which it indicates, combined with the insight it gives into the workings of the human mind in circumstances so different from ours.

AUNT HARRIET: Any one who has read Hiawatha will think of Pau-puk-keewis and the Gitchie Gumee or Big-Sea-Water, when he visits the Pictured Rocks.

> Then along the sandy margin
> Of the lake, the Big-Sea-Water,
> On he sped with frenzied gestures,
> Stamped upon the sand and tossed it
> Wildly in the air around him;
> Till the wind became a whirlwind;
> Till the sand was blown and sifted
> Like great snow drifts o'er the landscape,
> Heaping all the shores with Sand Dunes,
> Sand Hills of the Nagow Wudjoo.

THE PRESIDENT: There is a strong, though of course grotesque, relationship perceptible in some of these traditions with Scripture record. Hiawatha is himself of divine origin; he is the prophet and friend of humanity; he bears a commission to benefit his race. His mission ends when the Black-robed Pale-face comes to tell his people of the blessed Saviour. In one of his adventures we have an odd resemblance to the experience of Jonah. All this, with the avowed intention of the author to reproduce Indian traditions faithfully, makes Hiawatha worthy of special study for other reasons than for its delineations of scenery.

AUNT HARRIET: Undoubtedly, and I admire the happy way in which the poet manages to depict the more human features of the Indian character, bringing that race, so to speak, into the realm of our common brotherhood. But I presume we must not travel too far from Lake Superior.

MRS. MERRIMAN: There is a poem of Whittier's entitled "On receiving an eagle's quill from Lake Superior." To him, the sign speaks of the onward march of the American nation:

> The rudiments of empire here
> Are plastic yet and warm;
> The chaos of a mighty world
> Is rounding into form.
> * * * * * *
> Thy symbol be the mountain bird
> Whose glistening quill I hold.

ALBERT: And with this symbol before us, reminding us of the distance we are from our homes, and the necessity for bold and rapid flight, I will bespeak the power of an eagle's pinion for each one of our company for our southward journey, and so close our portfolio for this evening.

CHAPTER XV.

BOSTON AND THE WHITE MOUNTAINS.

WHEN the J. U. T. C. came together, as arranged, for their eighth meeting, at the house of Mr. Goldust, every member, as usual, was present; and, after the transaction of the routine business, the conversation was directed to the subject of the tour for the evening, namely, Boston and the White Mountains, the President taking the part of leader.

THE PRESIDENT: In any conversation or discussion about New England, no matter from what standpoint, it would be decidedly improper to leave out Boston; and so, in our wanderings hither and thither among the hills and valleys of New England, we shall do well to make Boston our rendezvous and point of departure. We can, however, only touch with exceeding brevity upon some of the features worthy of notice in that city. The view here given is of that part of Boston seen from Bunker Hill in the city of Charlestown, and looking out towards the bay. As you know, Boston is built upon an irregularly shaped peninsula, being in this respect somewhat akin to New York; but, unlike New York, the city limits are not confined to the peninsula, but reach over and include the adjacent lands and islands, with which it is connected by free bridges. Old Boston, however, was a much more restricted place, the various additions to the city having been made by annexation from time to time.

Bunker Hill monument, from which our view of Boston is taken, occupies the site of an old redoubt on Breed's Hill, famous in the annals of the War of Independence. It is a square column tapering towards the top, with a spiral staircase inside, and a small room just below the apex, from which a fine view is afforded. Perhaps we ought to pause here for an instant for a brief talk about the events of the stirring times commemorated by this simple but yet grand stone pile.

DR. PAULUS: As Americans we cannot but feel proud of the historic associa-

VIEW OF BOSTON.

tions of this spot. Here was fought out one of the sublimest conflicts that the world has ever seen. Of course, Boston had not all the struggle to herself, by any means; but she occupied a most conspicuous position in the history of that eventful period.

THE PRESIDENT: Let us try to realize something of the position of things on June 17, 1775. The American army, with their headquarters at Cambridge, under General Ward, at this time surrounded Boston, and the British, under General Gage, were cooped up in the city, with free access, of course, to the ocean. On the one hand, the Americans were bent on driving the British into the sea; and on the other, the British were determined to force back the Americans from their too close proximity. The British troops were well quartered, had abundant supplies, and were a fine, well-disciplined body of men. The Americans were raw militia, most of them fresh from their farms, with such weapons as they could command, and very moderately supplied with ammunition; but every man was fired with enthusiasm, and could be relied on to the last emergency.

Looking back across the century and recalling the memorable struggle of that bright June day, there mingles in my mind a feeling of sadness, with the natural emotion of joy at the ultimate triumph of the cause of liberty. Behind that double row of rail fences, stuffed with the new-mown hay from the Charlestown fields, were the descendants of men who by patient toil, by suffering and hardship, through blood and tears and fire and famine, had created a paradise out of a howling wilderness, and had handed it to their sons—a heritage of industry and virtue. A stupid king thousands of miles off, surrounded by proud and foolish nobles, instead of treating this bright and fair offshoot from England with the justness and frankness which it deserved, must needs set to work, inspired by senseless counsels, to harass and pinch and vex the new colony with unjust, meddlesome, and despotic laws. The patient toilers over the seas stood this as long as they could; but human patience has its limits, and it was absurd for George the Third to imagine that men who had sprung from such stock, and had such a record as the inhabitants of the American colonies, were going to be ruled by a foolish despot and a handful of haughty and disdainful nobles. Unfortunately, these nobles and their king were able to commit the people of England—the brothers of the colonists—to the cause of oppression, and, in the conflict which followed, brother was arrayed against brother.

DR. PAULUS: "Woe unto the world because of offenses! for it must needs be that offenses come; but woe to that man by whom the offense cometh."

THE PRESIDENT: Gilbert, can you give us very briefly the main incidents of the battle of Bunker Hill?

GILBERT: I will try, sir. The hasty entrenchments which you have described were on Breed's Hill, where the Bunker Hill monument now stands. This hill was part of a farm belonging to a Mr. Breed. A line of earthworks and a redoubt had been hastily thrown up during the night on the flanks of Breed's hill nearest Boston. General Prescott held this position on the morning of the 17th with a thousand men, who had toiled all night at the earthworks, and in the morning he was reinforced by General Stark, with five hundred men, and General Warren, of Boston, a physician soldier, and a man held in high esteem by his co-patriots. Dr. Warren took his station in the redoubt, and General Stark with his five hundred men lined the inside of the rail fences which extended from Breed's Hill to the Mystic River.

Meanwhile the British, led by Generals Howe, Burgoyne, and Pigot, landed at Morton's or Moulton's Point, with three thousand men—infantry, grenadiers, marines, and artillery. The soldiers were well under cover of the British ships in the harbor, and, as the boats landed the men, they were formed in companies, and then, sitting down on the grass, ate their dinners—for more than a thousand of them their last meal.

It so happened that the patriots at the rail fences stood the onslaught of battle. They well knew how to handle their shot guns, but they were short of ammunition. Three or four times did the British charge up the hill, and were received with such a raking fire, that whole columns were shot down. But as the day wore on, the American ammunition gave out. The war ships in the harbor had, in the mean time, succeeded in setting Charlestown on fire. The Americans fought for a time at their fences with the stocks of their guns, but column after column of British soldiers swarmed upon them, and they had to retreat, which they did at four o'clock in the afternoon. General Warren was killed at the redoubt towards the close of the battle. The American loss was 145 killed and 304 wounded; the British loss was more than double that of the Americans, and among the latter were thirteen commissioned officers.

The President: Thanks. It was not surprising that men who could hold their own for so long against so terrific an onslaught, soon rallied, and before long had the satisfaction of seeing the British leave Boston. Very soon after the battle of Bunker Hill, General Washington reached Cambridge, having been appointed by Congress to the command of the entire army. Washington saw the importance of the struggle at Boston, and came there in person to direct the movements of the Americans. His name was well known to every American soldier, and his arrival inspired the patriots with great confidence. Under his generalship Boston was so beleaguered and invested that on the 17th of March, 1776, General Howe and his army quitted the city, and the Americans took possession. And now, Miss Clara, will you be kind enough to give the club a brief historic explanation of what is sometimes called "the great Boston tea-party?"

Clara: If I understand it, the tea-party arose from a question of taxation. In Great Britain the principle was thoroughly recognized that the taxes to be paid by the people were to be decided by the representatives of the people. In other words, taxation and representation went together. In the colonies the people were taxed by the British Parliament, without having a voice in the matter. Perhaps the colonies would not have been in a hurry to fight over the *principle*, if the application of it had not become oppressive. But some of the Taxation Acts of Parliament were very heavy upon the Americans. I must ask the President to help me over the details, as to what some of the obnoxious taxes were.

The President: Give just what you remember.

Clara: Well, I know that one of these was called the Stamp Act, which was passed—

Bertram: March, 1765.

Clara: Almost every kind of legal document, notes, mortgages, etc., had to be printed on stamped paper made in England and costing from threepence to five or six guineas a sheet. Paper for newspapers, almanacs, pamphlets, etc., was taxed several cents a sheet, and every advertisement in a newspaper was taxed, I think, two shillings.

The President: How did this lead up to the tea-party?

Clara: It made a terrible commotion through all the colonies, and the act was finally repealed, but was soon after followed by an act compelling

A WHITE MOUNTAIN GLEN.

Americans to pay a duty on several articles of common use, amongst them being tea.

THE PRESIDENT: This was in 1767. In the mean time the great Mr. Pitt, who then sat on the Opposition side in the British Parliament, spoke firmly in favor of the colonies, and against the Stamp Act, and all similar attempts to tax the colonists.

MR. GOLDUST: Pray, what excuse did the British ministry make for taxing the Americans?

THE PRESIDENT: They thought that the colonists ought to reimburse England in some way for the expenses of the great French and Indian war, which was just over. It was as though England had taxed Canada during the war of 1812. If she had done so Canada would have replied: "If we are to pay you for defending us we will raise the money ourselves in our own way, but we will not let you come and take the money out of our pockets." They would probably have added: "You must remember that it is your own war, not ours, though it is fought on our borders." This was what the American colonists thought, and in effect said. They were willing to pay England money if she wanted it, but they would not let England come and take it by force without consulting them.

CLARA: But about the tea-party. When this new Taxation Act was passed there was another hubbub, of course, and Massachusetts now came to the front.

GILBERT: Was that why Boston is called *the Hub?*

CLARA: It might have been, but it was not. Massachusetts issued a circular calling upon the other colonies to unite in an effort to obtain redress of grievances. Riots took place in different parts of the country. The people of Massachusetts were declared rebels, and in Boston the soldiers shot down several citizens in the streets. This was in the spring of 1770, for these disputes and commotions lasted several years. At last the British Parliament agreed to take off all the obnoxious import taxes, *except that on tea.*

JOHN: The kettle now begins to boil.

CLARA: But, of course, this would not do. It was not now so much the tax as the *principle* which was objected to. No patriotic American would drink tea. A great deal of it was sent from England, but the people would not let it be landed, or else they stored it up in damp cellars and let it spoil. Some ships came to

MOUNT WASHINGTON AND THE WHITE HILLS.

Boston loaded with it. A great meeting was held in the town, and at its close fifty men, disguised as Indians, rushed to the wharves, followed by the crowd, boarded the ships, and emptied all the chests of tea into the harbor. That was the Boston Tea Party—16th December, 1773.

THE PRESIDENT: Excellently told, Clara. You know that, in retaliation for this, Parliament removed the Custom House from Boston to Salem, annulled the Massachusetts charter, and declared her citizens rebels; that a great Colonial Congress then assembled at Philadelphia to consider the situation, and that the other States unanimously agreed to stand by Massachusetts to the last. The king then sent a great fleet and an army of ten thousand men to whip the colonists into subjection.

And now, if you please, it is time for us to leave Boston and take the train to the White Mountains. We go to Portsmouth by the Eastern Shore line, passing Lynn, Salem, Marblehead, and Newburyport. At Conway junction we take the Mountain Division of the road, and pass Rochester, and so on to North Conway, which we may call the southeastern gate of the White Mountain domain, and whence we may direct our journeys as we please. As I have only a few views of this interesting region we will take them one by one and let them suggest to us such topics as they may.

MOUNT WASHINGTON RAILWAY.

The first view (p. 151) is of a general character, and I do not know that I can locate it. It is of a rocky glen, densely shaded, through which we must pick our way carefully. Perhaps some of you, in future rambles, may come across just this place; if so, you may recognize it by the curious bear-shaped rock on the right, like a bruin seated on its haunches.

In another picture we get an excellent view of Mount Washington and the White Hills. The summit of Mount Washington is 6,293 feet above the level of the sea, and is the highest point in this region, or in any place in America east of the Rocky Mountains, excepting some peaks among the Black Mountains in

SILVER CASCADE.

Carolina. The summit of Mount Washington is occupied as a meteorological station by the United States Government. There is also a summer hotel known as Tip-top or Summit House. On the east side of the mountain there is a carriage road, and on the west a railroad, either of which is very helpful to the tourist. The grade of this railroad is, in some places, one foot in three, and the track is of three rails, the center like a cog-wheel. The cars are swung so as to be always horizontal. Before these roads were built, the attempt to reach the summit was attended with considerable peril. In September, 1855, a lady who was accompanied by her uncle and cousin, died of fatigue and cold, and a pile of stones marks the place where her friends kept watch over her body through the long and sad night. There is also a spot pointed out where portions of a skeleton and some clothing were found in July, 1857. These were afterwards identified as the remains of a gentleman from Delaware. Dr. Benjamin Hall, of Boston, narrowly escaped with his life, after passing two nights on the mountain, lost in an October storm.

Mrs. Goldust: I cannot see why people should expose themselves to such risks. For my part, grand as mountains are, I like the lesser hills better.

Mr. Merriman:

"If thy heart fail thee, do not climb at all."

The President: Here is a view of a portion of Crawford's Notch. To reach this place it may be well to go to the Crawford House, one of the earliest hostelries in the White Mountains, and which can be reached by railroad from North Conway. As cars of observation are connected with the trains running through this region, it is pleasant to avail oneself of this means of travel whenever opportunity offers. The Notch is a mountain gorge, with walls 2,000 feet high, approaching in one particular spot to within twenty-two feet of one another. The brook Saco run through it, and the railroad also finds room. The Silver Cascade, of which our picture gives a view, is said to be the finest waterfall in the White Mountains. The fall is four hundred feet, almost perpendicular. There are numerous other cataracts, cascades, and objects of romantic interest which it would weary you if I were to try and describe. But our pictures speak for themselves in this respect.

CHAPTER XVI.

THE WHITE MOUNTAINS—CONTINUED.

COLONEL WARLIKE : Did I understand you as saying on a former evening, that the White Mountains formed a portion of the great Appalachian chain ?

THE PRESIDENT : No doubt. Speaking in a general way they do, as when classifying the leading mountain divisions of the continent ; but in subdividing these great ranges it is usual to put the White Mountains into a group with an older series called the Atlantic system, lying east of the Appalachians proper, and including the Maine mountains.

MRS. WARLIKE : What extent of territory is covered by the White Mountains?

THE PRESIDEN : About thirty miles from north to south, and 45 miles from east to west, and within this region there are over 200 distinct peaks, and innumerable mountain gorges, streams and rivulets.

GILBERT : I suppose the Indians had a name for these mountains ?

THE PRESIDENT : Yes, I find that they were called by the Indians Agiocochook, signifying "Mountains of the Snowy Forehead" and Home of the Great Spirit. It is somewhat curious that while a great many of the streams and lakes in New Hampshire retain their Indian names, it is very rarely that we find a mountain peak so honored. In this region the principal mountains are named after personages famous in our own history—Washington, Franklin, Monroe, Madison, Jefferson, etc.

I should say that the mountains are divided into two clusters, the western, called the Franconia Mountains, and the eastern, or White Mountains proper. Between these groups is a table-land or plateau of irregular shape, several miles in width.

I have here two very fine views, both from the Franconia group. One is of the Eagle Cliff Mountains, as seen from the Franconia Notch, looking northward.

There is a mingled softness and grandeur about this and the other view which

EAGLE CLIFF, WHITE MOUNTAINS.

is especially attractive. The Franconia Notch is a beautiful mountain pass, five miles long and half a mile wide. The sides are bold and often precipitous, and crowned with forests. The Pemigewasset River flows through this defile. There is a charming lake called Echo Lake near the north end, which ought to be visited. The echo from the center of the lake is wonderfully distinct, and of course there is the usual Indian superstition connected with it, that the echo is the voice of the Great Spirit. The second view is of the Cannon or Profile Mountain as seen from the Eagle Cliff Mountain, looking down the Notch. From some points of view the top of this mountain has some resemblance to a mounted cannon. The view from the summit is, of course, inexpressibly grand and very extensive. From another point of view the profile of an old man's face is distinctly traceable, and from a third, still another profile—that of an old woman. It was this mountain that suggested to Hawthorne his story in "Twice Told Tales" of "The Great Stone Face." Here we also find another beautiful lake called "Profile Lake."

LILIAN : Hawthorne begins his story, I think, by saying that the valley overlooked by this mountain contains many thousand inhabitants.

THE PRESIDENT : That is taking a kind of poetic license with these New Hampshire valleys, although some of them are quite populous.

ALBERT : I have read Hawthorne's little story, and I confess I do not see the point of it. It is of a simple-minded, virtuous man, growing up among his neighbors, and all his life looking for the fulfillment of an old legend that somebody will come along whose face shall resemble the profile of the "old man of the mountain," and that that person, whoever he might be, should be the greatest and noblest personage of his time. The people of the valley at length discovered that this simple-minded neighbor of theirs was the man.

THE PRESIDENT : I suppose that the moral lies in the fact that the man himself never suspected the likeness nor dreamed that he was either great or noble.

AUNT HARRIET : True nobility of character is, I suppose, inconsistent with what is termed self-consciousness or egotism.

THE PRESIDENT : The instant we begin to imagine we are great we betray our littleness.

DR. PAULUS: "Professing themselves to be wise they became fools."

AUNT HARRIET: Perhaps there is another point in the story. From habitual

CANNON-MOUNTAIN CLIFF, WHITE MOUNTAINS

contemplation of this natural object, and from associating it in his mind with thoughts of virtue, the man grew up in the moral likeness of an ideal character. Hence the value of an ideal, and of some outward things to remind us of it.

THE COLONEL: Is there not a touch of ritualism there, Miss Victor?

AUNT HARRIET: Possibly, but I am not ashamed of it if there is. Because ritualism may be carried to an absurdity by some people is no reason why we should not be taught through our senses.

BERTRAM: Professor, you must please tell us something of the geology of these mountains.

THE PRESIDENT: They are formed of the primitive metamorphic rocks, with peaks of granite and gneiss, but I have not yet read the reports of Professor Charles Hitchcock, the State geologist, which I understand are particularly full and valuable. Our time this evening will, however, hardly admit of an excursion into this branch of inquiry. Meantime I would ask if some member of the club can recite to us any portion of Whittier's poem on White Mountain scenery.

LAURA: I remember some lines of his from "Franconia."

"Once more, O Mountain of the North, unveil
    Your brows, and lay your cloudy mantles by;
    And once more, ere the eyes that seek ye fail,
    Uplift against the blue walls of the sky
    Your mighty shapes, and let the sunshine weave
    Its golden net-work in your belting woods;
    Smile down in rainbows from your falling floods,
And on your kingly brows, at morn and eve,
    Set crowns of fire! So shall my soul receive,
Haply, the secret of your calm and strength,
    Your unforgotten beauty interfuse
    My common life, your glorious shapes and hues
And sun-dropped splendors at my bidding come,
    Loom vast through dreams and stretch in billowy length
From the sea level of my lowland home.

CHAPTER XVII.

OTHER PICTURESQUE VIEWS OF NEW ENGLAND.

FOR our entertainment this evening, remarked the President, it is provided that we make short flying excursions to some other points in New England. And first we will have a talk about Connecticut and its famous river.

The history of Connecticut may be said to begin in 1630, when a grant of territory, extending from the southeast coast of Rhode Island, northward to the Massachusetts line, and westward to the extreme limits of the continent, was made to Lord Warwick by the Plymouth Company.

JOHN: What was the Plymouth Company?

THE PRESIDENT: A commercial and colonization company formed in England in 1606.

JOHN: The Puritans landed at Plymouth Rock in 1620.

THE PRESIDENT: This was, therefore, several years before the Puritans sailed for America. The Plymouth Company and the London Company were formed in England in consequence of discoveries in the western hemisphere, and for purposes of gain. They obtained Charters from King James I., and sent vessels over to America to settle the country and develop its resources for trade with England. The Plymouth Company were to operate north of the forty-first parallel of latitude. Take the map and note that this runs through New Jersey and Pennsylvania. The London Company were to operate south of the thirty-eighth parallel to the thirty-fourth, comprising part of Virginia, the Carolinas, etc. It would be interesting to follow the fortunes of these companies, but that is out of the question now.

MRS. GOLDUST: I always thought that the Puritans were the first white people that came to America.

THE PRESIDENT: By no manner of means; but they were the first that came *and stayed* in the part we call New England, and they stayed *to good purpose*, as

VIEW OF SALMON BROOK, GRANBY, CONNECTICUT.

you know. They were the actual *founders* of New England. Let me see—where were we starting from?

JOHN : The grant to Lord Warwick.

THE PRESIDENT: Oh yes! This was in 1630, ten years after the Puritans landed. A great deal had been done in those ten years. Besides the Puritan settlements in Massachusetts, the Dutch had founded New Netherlands, which ran right along the Hudson River, on both sides almost to Lake Champlain. Just about the time that the English Puritans sailed up the Connecticut River, the Dutch, advancing from the west, sent their settlers towards the same point, and for a time there was quite a little flurry as to who should possess the land. Finally, as you know, the English got it. It was a beautiful country, with hills and vales, rivers and streams, and fronting to the south on the grand Long Island Sound. If we had time, there are many lovely spots we might visit, but I dare not invite you to stay. Here is a view near Granby, in the center of the State of Connecticut, and here is another beautiful landscape, not in Connecticut, indeed, but in the noble valley of its river as it flows through Massachusetts under the shadow of Mt. Ascutney. Connecticut itself is full of lovely valleys and places of historical interest. From the time of the grant to Lord Warwick its settlement went steadily forward, slowly of course at first, encountering many difficulties, and the occasion of many political blunders and sins.

BERTRAM : How comes it that Connecticut is so small a State when its original grant gave it so much territory?

THE PRESIDENT: The original grantors did not take into consideration the Dutch settlement of New Netherlands, and in 1650 it was found necessary to come to terms with the latter colony, and to fix the boundary of Connecticut on this side of the Hudson, and subsequently the powerful Duke of York obtained grants from England, and New York absorbed New Netherlands. In fact, Connecticut soon found itself locked within its present rather confined but interesting and very beautiful territory.

We will now proceed farther north to the State of Vermont, where we find, first, a scene on the Missisquoi River.

CLARA : Indian name, of course.

THE PRESIDENT: **The Missisquoi** is, I suppose, the largest stream in Vermont,

MOUNT ASCUTNEY, CONNECTICUT VALLEY.

and the scenery through which it flows, and of which it forms an ever varying and delightful feature, is wild, charming and beautiful. To reach this river we should first make for the city of St. Albans, a fine town of some eight thousand inhabitants, and a few miles east of Lake Champlain. It is famous as the scene of a raid from Canada during the late civil war.

GRACE: I would like to hear about that.

THE PRESIDENT: I think that Mr. Merriman knows all about it.

MR. MERRIMAN: I remember it very well. There was a movement in 1864, on the part of the South, towards raising a disturbance on the Canadian frontier. It was a very natural thing, from a military point of view, to attempt. Some desperadoes seized two American ships on Lake Erie, and a small body of men, perhaps twenty or thirty, made a sudden raid into this little town, shot one or two men, robbed the banks of a good deal of money, and bolted back across the Canadian frontier with their plunder. It was an impudent thing, and the worst of it was that the Canadian judge who tried these rascals discharged them on some technical grounds, though the Canadian government had to make good the damages, as far as it could.

THE PRESIDENT: St. Albans was the rendezvous also of a Fenian army, 2,000 strong, in 1866. This army invaded Canada, but was quickly dispersed, and the foolish men were right glad to get passes from the American authorities on the railroad lines back to their homes again.

Eight miles from St. Albans is the delightful little watering place of Sheldon Springs, the waters of which are, I understand, much sought after. Here the Missisquoi flows through a charming valley with rich and romantic landscapes on every hand. Our view gives a portion of the rapids—a characteristic and truthful sketch.

Then we have a view of Mount Mansfield from Rice's Hill, an admirable picture of the northern portion of the Green Mountains. Mount Mansfield is the loftiest peak of this range, being about 4,400 feet high. On the whole, the tourist finds abundant material for enjoyment in this rural neighborhood.

MR. GOLDUST: I see that these mountains of Vermont do not have the rugged outline of the White Mountains, still less that of the Rocky Mountains.

THE PRESIDENT: No; they are of smoother and more rounded appearance, es-

VIEW ON THE MISSISQUOI RIVER, VERMONT.

pecially on the western slopes. At the termination of the long and severe winter they come forth clothed with a rich green grass, and this, together with the evergreen forests which abound on their sides, gives them their distinguishing name, which of course is the origin of the name of the State itself.

We now proceed by the quickest imaginary route to the little State of Rhode

MOUNT MANSFIELD, MASS.

Island, which, if modern researches are to be relied upon, is the ancient Vinland discovered by the Northmen about the year A.D. 1000. The view before us is of some rocks near Newport, and one of its principal natural objects of interest.

COL. WARLIKE: One of the finest fortifications in the United States is Fort Adams, at Newport.

NEGRO HEAD, NEWPORT.

THE PRESIDENT: Newport suffered very severely during the war of Independence. The British and Hessian troops quartered there were reckless and brutal in their destructiveness. In recent times it has become a fashionable and wealthy watering place.

MR. GOLDUST: Was not Rhode Island founded by Roger Williams, a Baptist minister?

THE PRESIDENT: Rhode Island obtained its charter in 1643 through Roger Williams, who in 1635 was banished from the Massachusetts colony for holding views which were then considered dangerous to the progress of the Commonwealth. He was a Baptist in principle, though up to the time of his departure from Massachusetts he was connected with the Orthodox Church of that colony.

LAURA: In what respects were the views of Roger Williams distasteful to the others?

THE PRESIDENT: Chiefly in this respect, that he denied the right of the magistrates and civil government of a State or nation to interfere or adjudicate on ecclesiastical or spiritual matters. The Puritans, though regarded as nonconformists in England, held decidedly Church and State sentiments. They believed in trying to *make* men good Christians by force of law, and frowned upon the broader views of Williams, who denied the right of the civil power to impose a religion upon a people.

ALBERT: Where did they banish him to?

THE PRESIDENT: It was their intention to send him back to England, but he gave them the slip, as the saying is, and with a few companions fled from his persecutors to the shores of the Narragansett bay, and, after a time, settled down among the Indians, purchasing lands from them, and calling the place Providence. He was a good man, of large intellect and heart, and the State of Rhode Island, though of necessity small, being limited in all directions by prior grants, or by the ocean itself, is a grand monument to his life and principles.

Our tour in this part of our country is of necessity a brief one, and must end here; for though modern science has almost annihilated such old-fashioned things as time and space, yet we cannot quite dispense with the supper-hour, which is now upon us. Perhaps on some future occasion we may do more justice to the Eastern States.

CHAPTER XVIII.

LAKE GEORGE.

LAKE George and the Adirondack region were at first chosen for successive tours. Owing to a slight misapprehension, two members had come prepared to lead the tourists through these very attractive fields of observation, on this, the ninth evening, at the house of the President. As this was expected to be the last but one of the regular meetings of the club, and as the tour for the tenth evening was already decided upon, it was agreed, after some conversation, to combine the two tours into one and to undertake them both. "This," remarked somebody, "is one of the advantages connected with this mode of traveling. We, are not bound by any of the fixed and definite rules of time or space, but can accommodate these to our wishes or dispense with them altogether."

Accordingly Miss Lilian was requested to conduct the club to a brief visit to Lake George.

LILIAN (*reading from notes*): Lake George is situated in Warren county, New York State, about sixty miles north of Albany. We reach it from Saratoga by rail to Glen Falls—to appreciate which spot, we must not only see it but read "The Last of the Mohicans,"—and thence by stage to Caldwell at the head of the lake. We pass by the spot where Col. Williams, the founder of Williams College, fell in battle, Sept. 8, 1755, and where a monument has been erected to his memory.

GILBERT: Col. Williams was leading his regiment on a reconnoissance of the French troops, when he fell into an Indian ambuscade and was shot through the head. It was found that he had willed all his property to the support of a free school, and this was the foundation of Williams College.

MR. MERRIMAN: The monument was erected in 1854 by the *alumni* of the college.

LILIAN: How can I begin to describe the charms of this lake and its surroundings, or bring before you the many interesting historic reminiscences connected with it? I hardly know how to begin, and I am afraid that I shall hardly know how to end. However, as our time is short, and as verbosity is forbidden by the

FOURTEEN-MILE ISLAND, LAKE GEORGE.

usages of this club, I will draw at once upon my portfolio, and while the pictures are being handed about I will "say my say."

First, let me inform you that this is not a little lake by any means. As compared with any of the great lakes of the north it is, of course, very small; but its thirty-six miles of length and its four miles of breadth at the widest, form no inconsiderable area. It is a good day's trip to go by steamer right along it and back the same day; from Caldwell on the south, to Baldwin on the north, where the lake finds its outlet, through Wood Creek, into the larger waters of Lake Champlain, some three or four miles distant.

Here there is a view of Fourteen Mile Island, or at least of a part of it. That is it, where the people are pushing off with their boat. I suppose there are steps cut somewhere in these rocks, so that we can climb up. This is a large island, and has a good hotel upon it. Before we get there we pass a good many points of interest, of which I will name a few. The general features of the scenery are the same of course as in the views now presented. There is a little island called Diamond Island, on account of the quartz-crystals found upon it. During the war of Independence a battle or skirmish took place on this island, and I am sorry to say that the patriots were beaten. Then there is Dome Island, where General Putnam once encamped his troops during the French war. In fact, it is astonishing how much history has been not written but *made* in this romantic region.

Of course you all know about the great French general Montcalm. We might spend the whole evening in following his footsteps (in imagination) over and around these waters.

MRS. GOLDUST: Please let us hear something about him.

LILIAN: He was a French marquis—Marquis de Saint Véran Montcalm—and a brilliant and successful soldier, trained to war from his youth, and dying on the battle-field of Quebec at forty-seven years of age, in the service of his country. He was general commander of the French troops during the French war in Canada in 1756–60. In 1757 he besieged Fort William Henry—the ruins of which we can explore at the south end of this lake—with 8,000 soldiers, and compelled the garrison of 2,500, including women and children, to surrender at discretion after a brave defense. But I am sorry to say he was either unable or unwilling, or, perhaps, both unable and unwilling to prevent the Indians who fought under him from barbarously massacring the entire garrison after they had given up their arms. This will always be a blot upon his memory. On the east shore of the lake is Ferris's Bay, where he marshaled his army and moored the boats in which he had descended the lake.

THE COLONEL: It was strange that both Montcalm and Wolfe, the two opposing generals, should be slain at that decisive battle on the plains of Abraham which fixed the destiny of America.

DR. PAULUS: And quite as strange the dying utterances of both men. Wolfe exclaimed, when he heard of the victory of his soldiers: "Then I die happy."

VIEW FROM FOURTEEN-MILE ISLAND, LAKE GEORGE.

Montcalm, on being told that he must soon die, said: "So much the better; I shall not live to see the surrender of Quebec." I have sometimes thought, if a human soul can be thus lifted above the fear of death by earthly emotions, how much more reasonable to believe in the triumph of the apostle Paul and of all believers as expressed in the words: "Thanks be unto God who giveth us the victory through Jesus Christ our Lord."

LILIAN: Here is another view from Fourteen Mile Island, and to vary the scene the artist has pictured it by moonlight with very grand cloud effects. How bold and sombre the rocks stand out in the foreground, and how beautiful the shadows on the rippling waters!

SABBATH-DAY POINT, LAKE GEORGE.

CLARA: That suggests the Indian name of this lake—Horicon, or silvery waters.

LILIAN: The steamer stops at a number of landing places on both shores, crossing and recrossing several times, giving many picturesque views. At length it enters the Narrows, passing by numerous islets, and with views of Black Mountains and Sugar Loaf Mountain on the east, and Deer's Leap Mountain on the west, and then we approach Sabbath Day Point, of which we have an illustration.

This spot, notwithstanding its peaceful name, was the scene of some hard fighting in the war of Independence. Just why and when it was first called by this

LONG ISLAND, LAKE GEORGE.

name no one seems to know. It is said that the British general Abercrombie halted here over Sunday with his troops in 1758, before proceeding to attack Fort Ticonderoga; but some authorities say that the place was known by its present name before 1758.

After leaving Sabbath Day Point we pass a rock called Anthony's Nose, and

Lake George. 177

two miles farther north Roger's Slide, and so on to Baldwin, where there are railroad cars in waiting to take the tourist northward to Ticonderoga and Lake Champlain. Going back by the steamer we will particularly notice two fine views, of which we have a representation—Long Island and the Cat Mountain.

GILBERT: I understand that Roger's Slide is so named because a Major Rogers,

CAT MOUNTAIN, LAKE GEORGE.

when pursued by Indians during the French war, slid down the rock. It was winter time and the water was frozen over, so that he contrived to escape over the ice.

MR. GOLDUST: That reminds me of the story of a hunter in California who thought to save time by sliding on a log down the face of a mountain. When half way down he espied a bear standing direct in his course, and eagerly watching him. The man was perfectly helpless, and, as he flew down, his log struck the bear—and bear, man, and log were carried headlong, in a medley, to the bottom. Finally the hunter had the pleasure of cutting up the bear and carrying his skin home, but it was a serious question at one time who would come out best, bear or man.

THE COLONEL : That is a good hunter's yarn, but quite as wonderful things do happen in the Sierra Mountains.

KATE : When was Lake George discovered?

LILIAN : By the French early in the 17th century, and it was named by the English after king George II. Its Indian name was Andiatarocte, or, "the place where the lake closes." The name "Horicon" is given it by Cooper, probably because the Iroquois tribe was sometimes called the Horiconi.

THE COLONEL : Does any member of the club know who this Major Rogers was of whom we have heard?

BERTRAM : He was Robert Rogers of New Hampshire. He offered to scout the woods with a battalion of men to be called rangers, and he saw some rare fighting.

AUNT HARRIET : I have listened with very great interest to these reminiscences, but at the same time I cannot express how sadly I feel when I associate these fair and lovely scenes with so much human bloodshed. It seems to me that the butchery of man by his brother man, when there is so much of sadness and misery in life without it, is a blot upon the human intellect. With life so short at best, and often so full of sorrow, the very thought of war and murder is appalling.

MRS. GOLDUST : The whole of creation is, according to the Apostle, groaning and travailing for redemption. I suppose humanity has not yet found what it seeks.

MR. HARVEY : What an inspiring thought that the wrong shall be righted and the mystery explained by and by.

THE PRESIDENT : "When the sword shall be turned into the plowshare and the spear into the pruning hook, and nations shall learn war no more."

THE COLONEL : To me that time seems farther off than ever.

AUNT HARRIET: I always enjoy singing the hymn:

"We are watching, we are waiting
For the bright prophetic day,
When the shadows, weary shadows,
From the world shall roll away.
We are watching, we are waiting
For the star that brings the day
When the night of sin shall vanish
And the shadows melt away."

DR. PAULUS: God grant that we may all see that day and rejoice.

MRS. MERRIMAN: It seems hardly possible, however, that war can ever again visit these peaceful scenes. For the present and for all the future they appear to be dedicated to peaceful occupation and the rest and refreshment of weary toilers. A hundred years does not seem so very long ago, and yet in that time the character of this region has been completely changed.

THE COLONEL: Greatly as I deplore the horrors of war, I sometimes think that it is by no means the worst enemy of mankind.

ALBERT: "Better to die with glory, than recline
On the soft lap of ignominious peace!"

The COLONEL: Exactly, and then we must remember that war, as an extreme resort, is often a national duty. It is a duty for the American government to defend the settlers on the frontier from the attacks of the savages. I admit, of course, the many wrongs which have been done to the Indians.

AUNT HARRIET: At least three-fourths of the wars that have arisen on earth have been disgraceful to the humanity and common sense of all concerned; but I cannot penetrate the mystery of sin, and I do not know that any of us can do more than simply let our lives, with whatever of influence they are crowned, preach forth the doctrine of love and brotherhood, and then hope in God for the rest.

LILIAN: Meanwhile, my dear Aunt, may we not rejoice in the glory God sends around us in these beautiful summer days of life? May we not draw from such scenes as we have been visiting a lesson of trust in the workings of Divine Providence, notwithstanding the gloom and the storm through which we must sometimes pass? I would like, before leaving this beautiful lake in its mountain setting, to quote a few verses from Whittier's "Summer by the Lakeside":

"O isles of calm! O dark still wood!
And stiller skies that overbrood
Your rest with deeper quietude!
*   *   *   *

"Farewell! around this smiling bay
Gay hearted Health and Life in bloom,
With lighter steps than mine, may stray
In radiant summers yet to come.

"But none shall more regretful leave
These waters and these hills than I:
Or, distant, fonder dream how eve
Or dawn is painting wave and sky;

"How rising moons shine, sad and mild,
On wooded isle and silvering bay;
Or setting suns beyond the piled
And distant mountains lead the day.
*   *   *   *

"O watched by Silence and by Night,
And folded in the strong embrace
Of the great mountains, with the light
Of the sweet heavens upon thy face,

"Lake of the Northland! keep thy dower
Of beauty still, and, while above
Thy solemn mountains speak of power,
Be thou the mirror of God's love!"

CHAPTER XIX.

THE ADIRONDACKS.

ILBERT: I dare not attempt to give you a description of the Adirondack wilderness, for I am not going to write a book; but I have half a dozen views which will occupy us probably during the rest of this evening.

You all know where to find this great region on the map. It is in itself almost a kingdom for extent, and its sovereign is Nature. It is too rugged, too wild, too far-off from the routes of business traffic, and perhaps of too little value in a mineral sense to become a "hive of industry." It is a vast, mountainous, lumbering, and fishing country, a hundred miles by one hundred and fifty in extent, and, a generation ago, was trodden only by the hunter, the trapper, and the lumberman. It has no sites in it for great cities; its rivers are mountain streams; its roads are bridle paths or tangled and rocky footways. Its carriages are the lightest of boats, one of which will carry two or three people on the lakes and streams, and can then be carried on the shoulders of a man until it is again needed, which will be before long, you may be sure. Its *hackmen* are *guides* at two or three dollars a day, *all found*. As travelers in the Adirondacks live mostly on the fish they catch and the deer they shoot down, the actual money cost of living per *head* is not very great. But then it is necessary that somebody in the party should know how to fire a gun and handle a fishing rod. Mere book-learning, college degrees, polished manners, and even money, will not suffice to obtain a meal for one hungry man, not to say several people. If ladies accompany the party, as they sometimes do, they must put aside the attire of the city and don a costume half Mohammedan and half modern—short dresses, Turkish drawers that fasten tightly at the ankle, thick boots, felt hat, buckskin gloves, and armlets to fasten tightly at the wrist. They will then be comparatively mosquito proof, a very necessary point—for even one mosquito or forest fly may prove a formidable enemy.

To those who cannot sleep except upon a regulation bed under a ceiling, and to whom the daily newspaper is a necessity of existence, there are hotels here and there in which the tourist can find everything to his hand; but to understand life in the Adirondacks one has to step outside of these conventional habits, to learn how to launch and paddle one's own canoe, to hunt, to fish, to build one's own camp at evening by some rippling brook, or on the shores of a still lake, to light a camp fire, and to sleep serenely, wrapped in a blanket, upon a couch of twigs. And it is wonderful how soon one gets not only accustomed to but even enamored of this sort of life. The days and weeks glide by; "the world recedes and disappears;" the stars become strangely familiar to us through the forest trees; the face and hands grow tawny; dyspepsia and headache fly away; and when the time comes for returning to civilization and business it is with no little regret that one turns away from this unkempt but salubrious and attractive wilderness.

I have here a beautiful picture of Preston Pond. Near by is a rugged Indian pass through which the hunters and trappers have long traveled from north to south. We may now consider ourselves in the very heart and center of the Adirondacks. Can you conceive of anything more solitary, stupendous, grand, and yet inviting to the tourist in search of these features in Nature? We have not here the ruggedness of outline of the Rocky Mountains, nor their immense elevation, and their eternal snows; and yet I do not know but that, in some respects, I prefer such scenery as this. These mountain peaks are high enough to climb for me. Some of them are over five thousand feet high, and there are five ranges of them—over five hundred mountains, and over a thousand lakes embosomed among them, with a vast, rugged, silent forest, seemingly immeasurable—that is to say, when you are living in it; and deer and other game innumerable, besides fish in plenty.

I do not know whether Longfellow ever spent a fortnight in the Adirondacks, but I think there is much force and feeling in his words—though I cannot speak from experience of any wearing sorrows or hard work:

> "If thou art worn and hard beset
> With sorrows that thou wouldst forget
> If thou wouldst read a lesson that will keep
> Thy heart from fainting and thy soul from sleep,

PRESTON PONDS.

Go to the woods and hills ! No tears
Dim the sweet look that Nature wears."

What do you say to that, Aunt Harriet?

AUNT HARRIET: From one point of view the poet is correct, but I do not altogether agree with him. Nature does sometimes wear anything but a sweet look, and to me she often brings thoughts of sadness, though I do not know that I love her the less on that account.

THE PRESIDENT: We go to Nature in all our moods for sympathy, and we get it. In the morning of life, or when the heart is full of joy and ecstasy, the flowers of the field, the trees of the forest, and the stars of heaven seem to rejoice with us ; and I think that in sorrow and sadness Nature is no less sympathetic.

CLARA : Is it not Mrs. Hemans who says :

"——An undertone
Was given to Nature's harp, for me alone
Whispering of grief."

GILBERT : St. Regis Lake, which is shown in our second illustration, is situated in the northwestern corner of the Adirondacks. There are two lakes of this name, upper and lower, and also a mountain peak ; and this is a favorite spot for hunters and fishermen.

ALBERT : What kind of deer are to be found in the Adirondacks ?

GILBERT : There are a few moose, but they are getting scarce. The common deer of the forest is like that shown in the picture. Let me see—it is called *Cariacus Virginianus.* It is over five feet long from nose to tail. It is a very beautiful, and in death a very useful animal. The venison is excellent eating, and its skin and horns are valuable. Its sinews are made into bow-strings and snow-shoes' netting. In the daytime it is hard to find, but at evening it comes to the streams and lake-side to drink, and so gets within range.

MR. MERRIMAN: There are game-laws regulating the hunting of this animal.

THE COLONEL: Oh yes. The hunting season lasts from September 1st to November 30—three months, and it is illegal to hunt them with dogs. They are said by hunters to be growing scarcer every year, though still fairly abundant.

GILBERT: Here is a charming view on the river Ausable, at a point near which it enters the upper Ausable Lake. This river with its branches flows in a general northeasterly direction through scenery of the wildest and most romantic character, and ultimately falls into Lake Champlain. There are some fine cataracts along this

DEER ON LAKE ST. REGIS—NIGHT.

stream, for instance the Alice Falls near Keeseville, and the Birmingham Falls (not a very romantic name) where it plunges over rocks seventy feet high, in a semicircle of great beauty. Then we come to the Horse-Shoe Falls, and so on to Ausable Chasm, a very picturesque spot, where the gorge narrows to a few feet, with high cliffs on each side, and glens with brooks and little cataracts branching out in all directions.

MR. GOLDUST: What are the principal fish caught in the Adirondacks?

MORNING ON THE AUSABLE.

GILBERT: Trout of all sizes, from small speckled trout to twenty-pound lake trout. You can find them in the stony mountain brooks, and among the lily-pads skirting the edge of the lakes and ponds, and large trout in June and July in the spring holes and deeper ponds. The best time to catch them is at sunrise and sunset.

THE PRESIDENT : That is a convenient arrangement for the tourist.

THE GLEN.

GILBERT : Certainly, as fresh trout from the lake or brook is no mean dish I assure you, especially with a mountain appetite for sauce.

MR. MERRIMAN : Does not Mr. Murray, in his famous book, speak of his experiences as an angler? I think he says that he caught a hundred brook trout in less than an hour, weighing from a quarter of a pound to two pounds and a half.

GILBERT: He must have had unusual luck.

THE COLONEL: You must go to the Maine forests if you would catch fine trout.

LAKE HENDERSON.

MR. MERRIMAN: It is several years ago since I paid my first and as yet only visit to the Adirondacks, in company with two friends. We found our way by a mountain wagon road from Ticonderoga to the northern end of Schroon Lake, and to Schroon River, where we stayed a few days at an inn kept by a man named Root— a real good fellow and a real good country inn. Mr. Root then drove us in a wagon and team to the head of Lake Sanford, which is the one spot in the Adirondacks worked by miners. The enterprise did not succeed, by reason chiefly, I believe, of the cost of transport, for there is, no doubt, plenty of iron ore. Here we stayed for a day or two and then tramped to Lake Henderson.

UPPER AUSABLE LAKE.

We crossed this beautiful lake in a scow, and made our way through the forests to the Preston Ponds, of which we have heard this evening, and in the neighborhood of which we stayed several days. I would like to repeat this tour with the same companions, or with any pleasant friends who enjoy out-of-door exercise.

GILBERT: Our last view is of the upper Ausable Lake. There is a great contrast between the upper and lower lakes of this name. The latter is grand and almost awful in some of its features. The mountains rise precipitously from the water's edge, sometimes six or eight hundred feet high, with streams and cataracts and many a gnarled and uprooted tree. The upper lake, on the other hand, nestles peacefully in the forest with gentle slopes receding from its banks, and distant mountains lending stately grandeur to the scene.

And now I must stop, for my portfolio is empty. I have not told you of the Saranac River and lakes, nor of the Raquette River with its magnificent lake from which it issues, and its course of a hundred and twenty miles to the St. Lawrence River; nor of a thousand other rivers, lakes, mountains, and valleys, which cover this glorious region. Neither have I time to speak of the natural history of the Adirondacks, its birds, its flora, and its geology. I must plead that my knowledge on these points is extremely limited; but if I should have the good fortune to address the club on a future occasion, I may have more information to impart on these interesting subjects.

The meeting then became informal, and after refreshments, music, and social converse, was in due season brought to a close.

CHAPTER XX.

THE HUDSON RIVER AND THE CATSKILLS.

HE tenth tour was held at the house of the President.

THE PRESIDENT: It falls to my lot to mention a few picturesque places on the Hudson, and to conduct you to the Catskill Mountains.

Almost from our starting point in New York, ascending the stream, we are impressed with the beauty and grandeur of the surroundings. On the left we soon reach the commencement of the peculiar rock formation known as The Palisades, from a fancied resemblance, I suppose, to a palisade fence. These Palisades constitute one of the most interesting features in the river scenery. They extend over twenty miles. There is an irregular columnar-like precipice springing from a sloping bank of shale and debris, the slope and the top of the ridge in some parts being covered with a forest.

The geologic features of this ridge have often puzzled geologists. The rock is granite—Lossing calls it a projecting trap dyke—lying upon a bed of sandstone, so that here we have a reversal of the usual order of things, the sandstone being a much later formation. To what freaks of nature, and to what period of time, this reversal of things is due, is an interesting topic which, with similar phenomena in other parts of the world, early arrests the attention of those who study geology. But the result in this instance is one which has been strikingly useful, for it so happens that these Palisades and the mountains of which they form the river frontage, furnish to New York city the stones which are used in her street pavements. The rocks are blasted, and then the blocks are hewn by chisel and mallet into cubes, or solid squares, and shipped by the contractors to the city. They make the very best of street pavements—the only one that will stand the immense traffic of the city, with its continual "tramp, tramp" of iron hoofs, and the ceaseless roll of countless wheels bearing merchandise and people along its thoroughfares.

I should state that these Palisades are in many places 300 feet high. Here

PINNACLES OF THE PALLISADES.

is a very fine view of one of the boldest portions of them, called "The Pinnacles."

If I were to attempt to give the historic features which make this river so interesting, I should have to expand this tour into several. Opposite the northern limit of the Palisades is Piermont, with its mile-long pier; and three miles south is Tappan, where Major André was executed. A few miles farther on the east side is Irvington, named after Washington Irving, and near by is Sunnyside, where he lived. Of course, every young American soon learns the place in literature filled by this pleasing author. His literary career extended over about the first half of this century.

Mr. Goldust: I was amused with the half contemptuous manner in which Thomas Carlyle disposes of Irving in his Reminiscences. He speaks of Irving being in Paris at the time Carlyle visited that city, says he was a kind of a lion at that time, and that he (Carlyle) had "a mild esteem of the good man." I think that is his expression.

The President: Carlyle had an unfortunate habit of writing down his own hasty and dyspeptic conclusions, as if they were more or less inspired, and he has tarnished his own grand reputation by so doing. He had a keen eye for the weaknesses of men, and in his brusque way, often held them forth to ridicule or condemnation, forgetful of their merits. I am sorry to say that we cannot, as I intended, have a little further conversation about this good man Irving.

The next point we come to in the order of our march is West Point, a place of great natural beauty on the west bank of the river. It is also of great national and historic interest and importance, besides being the site of a great military academy. I hardly like to pass Tarrytown by without a reference. We know that Major André was arrested here, Sept. 23d, 1780. Every American schoolboy knows the history of this man, and the circumstances attending his death.

Mr. Goldust: And I imagine that the idea of building a monument to his memory on American soil, however well intentioned, will never be tolerated by our people.

The President: I do not wonder at it. Admitting his courage and accomplishments, he aimed a most deadly blow, in the service of his sovereign, at American liberties, and it seemed almost a special interposition of Providence which frustrated his plans. There is this, however, to be said in extenuation of André; he never intended, when starting on his journey to meet Arnold, to enter the American lines as a spy. He was to meet General Arnold on neutral ground, and arrange the details of a surrender, proposed and planned by Arnold. The attempt to meet Arnold failed twice. Finally Mr. Joshua Smith, of Long Clove, just above Haverstraw, on the west bank of the river, went in a small boat in the night-time with two boatmen to the British ship *Vulture*, under a flag of truce, carrying a message to Major André, who returned with them, and met Arnold at Long Clove. After a long conversation together in the woods, André was anxious to return to the *Vulture*, but the two boatmen would not take him back. Possibly something had aroused their suspicions, although General Arnold's presence seemed to be a sufficient guarantee; but they pleaded danger, and stubbornly refused to go. So the principals adjourned to Smith's house, and there, over breakfast, completed their plans for the surrender on September 26, four days later, of West Point, the key of the Hudson and the great stronghold and storehouse of the Americans. This was Sept. 22d. During the forenoon Arnold entered his barge and sailed up the river to his headquarters. André waited until evening and then, accompanied by Mr. Smith, crossed the Hudson at Stony Point by the regular ferry, and with Arnold's pass, made out in favor of John Anderson, in his hand, went through the American lines on the east side of the river. Smith here left André, and the latter pursued his way alone on horseback. Coming to a fork in the road he turned to the right through Sleepy Hollow, and when within half a mile of the British outposts fell into the hands of three patriots, who stopped him and discovered in his boots some treasonable papers which he had obtained from Arnold.

MR. MERRIMAN : What were Arnold's motives in planning this treachery?

THE PRESIDENT : It is hard to fathom them. He was doubtless chagrined at having been censured for some irregular action in the army, and on account of the failure of some claims of his upon Congress. Perhaps also he miscalculated the issues of the contest, and was desirous of being on the winning side. At any rate he showed himself to be utterly without principle, although he had previously fought well and earned distinction as a soldier.

We now steam up the river, passing Stony Point with its history, also leaving Peekskill on the east, and grand old Donderberg—Thunder Mountain—on the west. Anthony's Nose is also seen to our right—a very prominent feature in the landscape, the meaning of which is duly set forth in Irving's curious " History of New York." We are now going through the Highlands of the Hudson and in the midst of the most picturesque scenery. We pass Iona Island, with its vineyards, and (on the right) Sugar Loaf Mountains and Fort Independence. Buttermilk Falls come into view on the left, and then West Point.

LILIAN : You have omitted Clinton and Montgomery forts, and have said nothing about the old chain or boom across the river at this spot.

THE PRESIDENT : Simply because we have not time to refer, even in passing, to all the interesting places. The scenery at West Point is very beautiful, and it would pay us to land and ascend to the ruins of old Fort Putnam, which can be seen on the heights from the river. Bull Hill and Breakneck Hill, and other features of the landscape come and go. We pass Fort Constitution on the right, Cornwall landing and Newburg on the left, Poughkeepsie on the right, and opposite this beautiful city we see New Paltz landing, at which, if we so please, we can disembark, and proceed by stage to the charming Lake Mohawk, where we may very enjoyably pass a few days before extending our trip to the Catskills.

These mountains cover a territory of at least thirty miles square, comprising, of course, numerous towns and villages. Geologically they present the same general features as the Alleghanies of Pennsylvania ; but they differ from the latter in the important particular that the peculiar dips in the strata shut out the possibility of coal beds being discovered. The Catskill region will never, therefore, possess a mining character. It will remain for all time a roaming ground for the tourist in search of health and recreation, the botanist, the artist, and the lover of nature. Many of the mountains are clothed with forest: but over vast tracts the hills stand out in desolate and naked outline, enclosing plateaus in which villages have sprung up for the entertainment and care of the tourist. From these places excursions to different points of interest are organized—sometimes on foot, sometimes in carriages. But it is now impossible for us to visit a tithe of the sights worth seeing.

Here is a glimpse of a view from Sunset Rock, which suggests Wordsworth's descriptive lines :

" O, 'twas an unimaginable sight !
Clouds, mists, streams, watery rocks, and emerald turf,
Clouds of all tincture, rocks and sapphire sky,
Confused, commingled, mutually inflamed,
Molten together, and composing thus
Each lost in each,——
*   *   *   *
' Below me was the earth : this little vale
Lay low beneath my feet ; 'twas visible—
I saw not, but I felt that it was there."

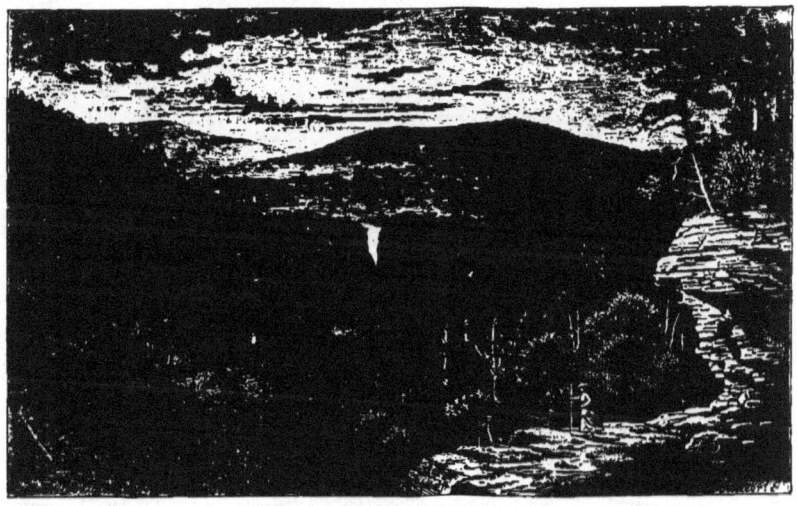

SUNSET ROCK, CATSKILL MOUNTAINS.

We have two more cuts illustrating different features of Catskill scenery, and with these we must close this series of tours. The Artist's Grotto is a water-worn cave, well worth a visit. The other scene is suggestive of a hundred different ravines, where the mountains are hidden from sight, and where—the rippling waters at our feet, and the forest about us and above us—we may drink to the full of the enjoyment of solitude.

ARTIST'S GROTTO, CATSKILL.

Among many pleasure-trips in this region, I would remember a walk or ride from Palenville up the new turnpike road to the Hotel Kaaterskill—two hours of steady climbing, gorge after gorge, hill after hill, until the great hotel on the crest of the mountain comes into view, with its crowds of visitors sitting on the broad piazzas, or walking on the noble terraces, in full enjoyment of the rare and breezy atmosphere, and of the magnificent views, and the whole bursting upon one, after the solitary pilgrimage, like a fairy creation or a new world.

I shall never, too, forget the drive from Tannersville to Phœnicia, through Stony Clove, a great rift fifteen miles long, through mountains three or four thousand feet high. Here the air was delightfully cool on the hottest day of a hot season, no damp, and no mosquitoes either. In some of the deeper crevices thin layers of ice were found by the more enthusiastic and diligent searchers.

Another ever-to-be-remembered trip, was by Pelham's Four Corners up the ravine of Rip Van Winkle, the Sleepy Hollow of the Catskills, past the spot said to be the scene, as depicted by Irving, of poor old Rip's long sleep—and so on, slowly, by the mountain and forest road, to the White Mountain House. On this trip we encountered a heavy rain and thunder storm, in which the reverberations and rolling echoes of the thunder among the hills were inexpressibly grand ; but we were thankful, as we neared the summit, to see the clouds roll away, to catch glimpses of the evening sunlight through the foliage, and to hear again the twittering of the birds.

And now the time has arrived for bringing these pleasant entertainments to a close.

"Harp of the North, farewell! The hills grow dark,
On purple peaks a deeper shade descending."

We have had many a pleasant ramble over mountain, prairie, valley, and woodland, and have gained, I hope, not only pleasure, but information and mental stimulus from our excursions. Let us cherish these pleasant memories, that they may suggest to us good and helpful thoughts in the path of life yet before us. ·And I do not know that I can better express my feelings or yours in closing this

A CATSKILL BROOK.

volume of our adventures than by quoting from one of Mrs. Hemans's sweet songs :

> " There's beauty all around our paths, if but our watchful eyes
> Can trace it midst familiar things, and through their lowly guise;
> We may find it where a hedgerow showers its blossoms o'er our way,
> Or a cottage window sparkles forth in the last red light of day.
>   * * * * *
>
> " With shadows from the past we fill the happy woodland shades,
> And a mournful memory of the dead is with us in the glades;
> And our dream-like fancies lend the wind an echo's plaintive tone
> Of voices, and melodies, and of silvery laughter gone.
>   * * * * *
>
> " Yet should this be? Too much, too soon, despondingly we yield !
> A better lesson we are taught by the lilies of the field !
> A sweeter by the birds of heaven—which tell us, in their flight,
> Of One that through the desert air forever guides them right."

www.ingramcontent.com/pod-product-compliance
Lightning Source LLC
Chambersburg PA
CBHW020909230426

43666CB00008B/1383